BETWEEN FRIENDS

Roger Royle's life has been dominated by two intertwined vocations: a priest and a broadcaster/writer. His priesthood has called him to serve in parishes, cathedrals, hospitals, homes and schools. His role as a broadcaster/writer has put him in contact with people throughout the world, most of whom he has never met and many of whom have little or no connection with organized religion. However, he has tried to keep these two vocations working in tandem so as to reflect a strongly-held belief that there is no such thing as sacred and secular. All is sacred.

Between Friends is a small collection of pieces he has written for *Woman's Weekly* magazine over the years. Hopefully they reflect that belief.

I would like to dedicate this book to two young gentlemen who are never likely to be *Woman's Weekly* readers but mean a great deal to me, their great uncle, Tomás and Pablo Camprubi.

Between Friends

Roger Royle

Published in Great Britain in 2000 by
Society for Promoting Christian Knowledge
Holy Trinity Church
Marylebone Road
London NW1 4DU

British Library Cataloguing-in-Publication Data

A catalogue record for this book is available from the British Library

ISBN 0-281-05374-X
Typeset by David Gregson Associates
Printed in Great Britain by Mackays of Chatham

Contents

May I thank all the readers of *Woman's Weekly*, many of whom have become friends over the years. But I would especially like to thank the staff of *Woman's Weekly*, the editors Gilly Sinclair, Olwen Rice and Judith Hall and the subs who have looked after me, Wendy Stacey and Sue Wallman, and particularly the editor's secretary, Susan Eames, who has coped with constant calls.

Thank you also to Elizabeth Marsh, and the staff of SPCK, who asked me to compile this collection.

Introduction

For nearly 20 years week in, week out, I have written a column for a woman's magazine. Sometimes a whole page, sometimes half a page, sometimes only 100 words but I have been there, accompanied by a photograph which, fortunately, hasn't aged as quickly as I have.

It hasn't all been plain sailing. There have been times when I have been asked to rewrite my article. There have been some articles that have never seen the light of day. Once I even got the sack. But then so did the vet. Fortunately, due to reader pressure, we were both reinstated.

For the past ten years I have been with *Woman's Weekly*, starting as 'The man who sees', and now on the letters page as a friend of the readers. It is a great privilege. At one time there were many clergy writing for the different titles, people such as David Sheppard and Bryan Green, but now there are very, very few of us left.

Somehow it is assumed that I do the Problem Page but that is not true. Whenever I am asked which column I write for *Woman's Weekly*, I say I do the 'Uplift Column'. Hopefully each week I write something that will sustain the spirit, uplift the mind and nourish the soul. Needless to say, I don't always succeed. There have been times when I have thoroughly annoyed some readers, driven others to distraction and confused others, but they haven't been slow to tell me. Letters from India, Australia, Canada, along with ones from all over the UK, arrive regularly at the *Woman's Weekly* office, and thanks to the diligence and devoted care of the editor's secretary, Susan Eames, are sent on to me. Fortunately very few are abusive, although quite a few are hard hitting. On a postcard I do my best to reply.

The readership is large and varied. I am writing for some people who have believed in God for a lot longer than I have, who are very mature in their faith. I am also writing for people who are searching, some who have little or no time for organized religion as well as for people of faiths other than the Christian faith. All this needs to be borne in mind when, in the early hours of the morning, I put pen to paper or rather finger to keyboard.

The other thing I have to remember is that *Woman's Weekly* is a secular magazine. This excites me. I have never wanted to be part of what can be seen

1

as ghetto writing or broadcasting; a Christian writing for other Christians. Obviously there is a place for that but I prefer to be where I believe Jesus Christ was when he did a lot of his teaching, in the market place, in the countryside, in the home. In his teaching he took nothing for granted and so he talked about everyday things, lost coins, wheat and weeds, sowers, lost sheep, rebellious sons and mugged travellers. I have done my best to follow that example with *Between Friends*. Again, I haven't always succeeded. But if the God who became man could take ordinary situations and draw from them spiritual understanding, then I think we ought to try and do the same.

Even if you have read these pieces before, I hope you will enjoy rereading them. For those of you who come fresh to them, I trust you will not be left spiritually hungry. I hope you will want more!

1

Times and Seasons

Just before his ascension into heaven, Jesus told his disciples, 'It is not for you to know the times or seasons the Father has set by his own authority.' Both the passing and the marking of time have been very important to the whole human race. Possibly now more than ever.

Less than 20 years ago you hardly ever knew when someone reached their fortieth birthday, but now banners are put on motorways, flags are fixed to roundabouts and balloons are attached to gateposts. All so that you may know that Tom, Dick or Tracy is 40.

At one time the rhythm of the Church's year would have given a good enough reason for rejoicing. But as organized religion loses its hold on society, secular feasts have to be found and what better than someone's 40th birthday.

It was the passing of time that formed the framework of the Creation stories in Genesis: 'And there was evening and there was morning, the first day.' Forty, whether days or years, was seen as a significant number, as was three. We are told that Abraham lived until he was 175, his wife Sarah until she was 127, and Joseph only made it to 110. Mind you, they were all outstripped by Noah's grandfather, Methuselah, who according to Genesis was 969 when he died. If some scientists have their way some of us will be on this earth nearly as long. Scientists don't seem to be interested in the life hereafter. It is the here and now that means most to them.

The psalmist scaled down our lifespan, and he wasn't that encouraging about what was left. 'The length of our days is seventy years, or eighty, if we have the strength; yet their span is but trouble and sorrow, for they quickly pass and we fly away.' Someone must have upset him that day!

Times and seasons are important. We need to be able to mark the passing of time. To keep both our body and soul healthy, we need a certain pattern of feasts and fasts as well as good old run of the mill time in between.

Time is like an ever rolling stream. It gives life, it takes it away. What matters is the way in which we use the time we're given. It might of course be easier if we knew how long we had, but we don't. So don't waste time. Get on with it.

3

Special occasions

As a child, the moment I got home having had a new suit, shirt or shoes bought for me, I wanted to wear them. The fact that they'd been bought for a special occasion didn't bother me two hoots. They were mine and I wanted to look good. My mother thought otherwise. They were to be kept for best and only brought out on high days and holy days.

I was reminded of those battles Royle when I passed a pub with a sign saying 'Full Sunday lunch, all day, every day'. Sunday lunch always was, and still is, rather special to me. It had to be roast beef, Yorkshire pud, roast potatoes, two veg and Nanny's apple tart. It was also the day that we would all sit down to lunch together as a family. These days the menu may have changed, and I rarely sit down with my own family, but I often enjoy the company of other families and friends who invite me to share a special meal with them.

But how on earth can it be special if it's available all day, every day? It can't be. Somehow we seem to have lost the sense of the special, and with it dragged down the standards of life.

The reason why the Christian Church today has its seasons, Saints' days and festivals is to bring changes into what might otherwise be a routine life. If variety is the spice of life, why do we spend so much time trying to make everything the same? Even Sunday is no longer special. I know it was often a dull day for some, but now it's just like any other day, only in some places worse. You no longer have to wait until autumn for chrysanthemums; strawberries are no longer just a summer fruit, and Easter eggs and hot cross buns can be bought 365 days of the year. It's no wonder that people look for dangerous ways in which to bring excitement into their lives.

We need variety. We need to keep some things special, some things for best, if only for the sake of our spiritual well-being. Otherwise dullness and drabness will dog us.

Signs of the times

There are certain times when I believe that the old saying 'Red sky at night, shepherds' delight; red sky in morning, shepherds' warning' is as accurate a weather forecast as anything that comes from the meteorological centre. Still, with global warming and the increasingly unsteady state of our planet, it can't be an easy job predicting our weather. Signs in the sky were very important to our ancestors. They often used them as guides to action. In fact, their whole lives could be controlled by portents over which they had no control.

Their lives were simple. Their education was basic. In the Old Testament, Moses believed the burning bush was a sign from God. Joseph interpreted the plagues in Egypt in the same way. The prophets were constantly looking for and divining signs they believed God had sent to warn the Children of Israel to turn from their wicked ways.

In the New Testament we're warned against signs. When the religious leaders try to test Jesus by asking for a sign from heaven, he is recorded as 'sighing deeply'. He pointed out that it was only a wicked and adulterous generation that looked for signs and the only sign they would be given was the sign of Jonah. In other words, they had to put their old lives behind them and start anew.

The trouble is that today, with our complicated lives and our advanced state of education, we still look for portents. We allow our lives to be controlled by the whims and fancies of our superstitious minds.

But what God is looking for in each one of us is not superstition but faith, a faith that thinks deeply about our beliefs and trusts that God, whose children we are, will care for us in good times and bad. Superstition holds us back. Faith sets us free.

Time to deliver

It's perfectly possible to put a man on the moon so why is it impossible for shops to be precise about delivery times?

Gas and electricity companies are just as bad. And as for the new privatized delivery firms, well the least said the better. They seem affronted by the fact that you're not in when they call, as though you've nothing else to do but wait around for them all day.

Still, such matters have caused consternation from time immemorial. I believe that some people arranged to be in Jerusalem so that they were in prime position for either the end of the world or the Second Coming of the Lord, which they believed would take place at midnight on 31st December 1999. Somehow or other, they worked out that God would use the new millennium's arrival to make his mark.

They may well be proved right but I doubt it. When people questioned Jesus about times or places, he told them, in effect, to mind their own business.

When his disciples, just before his Ascension into Heaven, asked him, 'Lord, will you at this time restore the Kingdom to Israel?', he replied, 'It is not for you to know times or seasons which the Father has fixed by his own authority.'

They should have known better than to ask such a question. After all, when Jesus taught his disciples about the Second Coming, he'd warned them, 'But of that day or that hour no one knows, not even the angels in heaven, nor the Son, but only the Father. Take heed, watch; for you do not know when the time will come.' And he ends by saying, 'What I say to you, I say to all: Watch.'

So perhaps I shouldn't be so critical of shops and services. After all, they seem to be training us for the Second Coming. We just need to be ready and waiting. It could happen at any time.

Changing times

Thanks to the RSPB, English Nature, The Harewood Estate and Yorkshire Water, red kites, a once common bird of prey, are back in Yorkshire. I just hope that this time they're treated better by the local clergy. During the last century, red kites were almost exterminated because the clergy decided that they were unclean and therefore a health hazard. They encouraged their parishioners to spend their Sunday afternoons knocking their nests out of trees. Imagine that happening today! There would be protest groups outside every church, and rightly so. But doubtless the clergy, at the time, thought they were doing the right thing.

But then look at butter, sugar, wine and eggs. All have gone in and out of fashion. Even the thought of putting lashings of butter on your toast now brings you minutes away from a heart attack. And as for 'going to work on an egg', well, in the eyes of some that must be considered one of the most dangerous modes of travel!

The Bible may well encourage us to 'take a little wine for thy stomach's sake' but today's nutritionists can't make up their minds whether it strengthens your blood or destroys your brain. It's all very confusing.

Fads and fashions have always changed, and that's a good thing. No one's thinking should stand still. But our fads and fashions will only stand up if our foundations are secure. Fads and fashions are interpretations; foundations are the whole truth.

Foundations are such things as faith, hope and love. Faith needs to be an integral part of everybody's life. How that faith is expressed has changed over the ages. A person can't survive without hope. And yet the hopes we have are far more adventurous and demanding than our parents ever had. Without love a person doesn't live; they just exist. The way in which love is now shown is so much more complicated, and in many cases far fuller, than it would have been, say, a century ago.

If the foundations are secure, they can withstand any fads or fancies. People will always see through the shallow ones and hang on to those of value.

Serving time

The watch strapped on your wrist and the clock on the wall can be cruel masters. Although I know time drags for some people, for most of us it has a habit of catching up with and even overtaking us.

As a result, we often long for more hours in the day and more minutes in the hour. And yet, if our wish could be granted, how would we spend our extra ration? Some of it might well be put to good use but far more would probably be squandered.

What's needed is a different attitude to using the time we've got. We shouldn't split our time into sections, setting some aside for work, some for family, some for home and some for ourselves. It would be far better to treat it as a whole, to be engaged with every moment. For all time is precious.

Sitting down with a good book can be an enriching experience, but I find some far more improbable activities equally absorbing. For instance, it may seem incredible but for me, even the time spent ironing can be fulfilling. Because I'm not particularly fussy about the standard of the finished article, I use the time to think or even pray. I may end up with too many creases in my shirt but at least I've managed to smooth out some of the creases in my soul.

I also enjoy the time spent preparing a meal as much as the time spent eating it. Kitchens are famous for good conversations and the discussions that take place there can be even more stimulating and lasting than those at the table.

If we stubbornly stick to the view that only certain set-aside times are of any worth, we're in danger of missing the true value of the hours spent simply getting on with life. And after all, that's how most of us do spend our time.

This thought is summed up in the lovely simple hymn: 'Teach me my God and King in all things Thee to see; And what I do in any thing, to do it as for thee.'

In the fourth verse we are told: 'Who sweeps a room as for thy laws, makes that, and the action, fine.'

In other words, all time is to be valued, for all time is God's.

Born leaders

It's no wonder *Dad's Army* remains one of television's most enduring sitcoms with characters such as Captain Mainwaring in it. Crisis and chaos are only minutes away and yet he sees himself as a born leader, able to tackle any problem, great or small. Even when Corporal Jones is running round shouting, 'Don't panic!', self-doubt never enters Mainwaring's mind. He was born to lead and lead he will. But as with so many people, it's a case, in Jesus' words, of the blind leading the blind.

Leadership is an awesome responsibility. Moses found it none too easy getting the Children of Israel through the wilderness, and Jesus had his problems explaining to his disciples what was expected of them. But at least both of them knew where they were going and how they were going to get there.

You may not see yourself as a leader, but if you're a parent you certainly are. Your children look up to you. They need guidance. It's in the home that standards are set, and if there's little leadership there, then heaven help the child.

Children are the best mimics imaginable. What they see, they copy. So if parents have a clear idea of where they're going, their children feel secure, knowing exactly what's expected of them. Later on in life they may come across teachers, colleagues or bosses who inspire them, but the foundations are laid in the home at an early age.

If children can't trust their parents, there's small hope they'll trust anyone else. If parents show no interest in their children, then there's little chance that the children will show any interest in themselves or others.

Parents have a responsibility to lead their children: it's part of the job. Taken seriously, it's the most fulfilling experience anyone can have.

As we mark Mothering Sunday, we should ask ourselves what could be more creative than shaping a new life?

Too early for tests

There are times when I think politicians live on a different planet from the rest of us. Certainly the latest idea of 'tests for toddlers' seems strange to me. What has happened to childhood? Children have to face competition soon enough. Their early years, though vitally important, should be free from that sort of stress. Even if tests don't feel too stressful to the children, I'm sure they will to their parents, and stress can be easily passed on.

Children have so much to explore, so much to experience, that they should be allowed to do just that and, what's more, enjoy it. These days, their trust, innocence and sense of well-being disappear horribly quickly anyway, without their being subjected to tests.

Childhood is a mystical time. A new life is being shaped and foundations are being put in place. Surely this can be done without tests? One of the most beautiful pictures of childhood in the Bible comes from the prophet Isaiah. The Prince of Peace is to be a child, 'For to us a child is born, to us a son is given ... and his name will be called Wonderful Counsellor, Mighty God, Everlasting Father, Prince of Peace.' Continuing his vision of peace, Isaiah writes, 'The wolf shall dwell with the lamb, and the leopard shall lie down with the kid and the calf and the lion and the fatling together, and a little child shall lead them.'

When Jesus is asked by his disciples, 'Who is the greatest in the kingdom of heaven?', he immediately calls a child, puts him in the midst of them and says, 'Truly I say to you, unless you turn and become like children, you will never enter the kingdom of heaven.' He also has very stern warnings for those who abuse children or lead them astray.

Innocence is soon lost. Trust is easily put under strain. A sense of well-being is quickly called into question. Childhood is so precious that we must do all in our power to preserve it. I'm not sure that tests for toddlers will help.

Help the aged

You may call it self-interest, but now I've had my 60th birthday I'm interested in pensions, nursing homes, sheltered housing and concessions for senior citizens. And I'm not alone. Many parts of the world have an ageing population and we crinklies are becoming expensive to look after.

But it's very sad when the elderly are seen as a burden. These days it seems few parents encourage their children to respect older people. I was on a train when two elderly ladies got on. They weren't very steady on their feet, yet not one of the children sitting got up and offered them a seat. And their parents didn't tell them to.

In many societies, especially in the so-called underdeveloped ones, the elderly are still held in great regard. They're seen as the people who hold the family together.

Certainly the biblical tradition is to honour the elderly, as it is in many other faiths. It's true the Old Testament writers may have had a different way of calculating age. It's hard to believe Abraham was 175 years old and Noah 500 when he fathered Shem, Ham and Japheth, and Methuselah reputedly reached the ripe old age of 969. The point is that their contribution to society was highly valued.

When Jesus was first brought to the Temple, it was two elderly people, Simeon and Anna, who recognized him as the Messiah. Throughout the Bible, the elderly are respected for their wisdom, advice and experience. They're kept within the family and are listened to. I'm sure it can't always have been convenient but it was seen as a duty.

Obviously our way of life has changed from biblical times. We don't live in small communities. There aren't always the space and facilities in a modern house to care for someone of another generation, but that doesn't mean the elderly should be forgotten or dumped on a scrap heap. We should rediscover our respect for them as vital members of the human family.

Showing respect

Drawn by the many delights of those delicious dairy products that are supposed to be so damaging to your health, I spent a week touring Normandy this summer.

In between the distinctive tastes of Camembert with butter on a baguette, washed down by a draught of local cider, I tried to balance my trip with the odd visit to a château, castle or cathedral.

On the Sunday morning I was in Caen. I decided to worship at St Peter's, in the town centre, a church that suffered terribly during the 1939–45 war but which has been wonderfully restored.

I arrived a little early so as to look at the beautiful building before the service began. As I wandered around, I overheard two English voices with distinct Northern accents. I went across and started to talk with them.

They were an elderly couple having a rather special holiday. The last time the man had been in Normandy was as a young soldier in 1944. He wanted to show his wife those places where he and his mates had seen fierce fighting. He had lived to tell the tale; many of the others hadn't. This brought us to the subject of the war grave cemeteries that feature so prominently in Normandy.

'They are a very moving sight,' I said. 'Places of great dignity and beautifully kept.'

'No better than they should be,' was the blunt Northern response. 'After all they did for us, they deserve to be treated with dignity and respect.'

The last world war was more than 50 years ago but the Falklands, the Gulf and Northern Ireland have all claimed their victims more recently. The sacrifices made by many should never be taken for granted. Laying down one's life for a friend is the greatest act anyone can be called to make.

Because we demand to be protected we have a duty to respect those who have been, and are, prepared to pay the ultimate sacrifice.

Respect and sacrifice are two words not much used these days. As we approach the annual time of Remembrance, perhaps we should consider using them a little bit more.

The power and the glory

Although Herod was a puppet king, put there by the Romans, he was determined to show who was in charge. Power had gone to his head and heaven help anyone who tried to undermine or question that power. No wonder then that, when the three wise men arrived from the East, they were unwelcome visitors.

In asking after a baby born to be King of the Jews, they threatened Herod's very existence. Astrologers were summoned, courtiers questioned, but no one could come up with a satisfactory answer. So the wise men were encouraged to go on their way to Bethlehem and, having found the King, to return to Herod so 'he may come and worship him also'.

When people want power, they will stop at nothing. Herod had no intention of worshipping Jesus. All he wanted was his destruction and he would go to any lengths to achieve it. The slaughter of the innocents must be one of the most brutal acts in history. Herod is a prime example of the corruption that power can bring.

If palaces are for the powerful, then stables are for the servants. And yet it was in a stable that a baby was born who was destined to have more power than any earthly ruler. This was the baby who grew up to attract millions of men and women to follow him. If that isn't power, I don't know what is.

Unlike Herod, Jesus never claimed power for himself. His power came from his Father. It was God the Father who gave him the strength he needed and it was his Father's glory he reflected.

The power that was with him as a baby remained as he became a servant and washed his disciples' feet. For power doesn't come with position. It comes with knowing that you are a child of God and draw your strength from him. Only those who are humble have real power, the power from which God's gift of glory comes.

Take off the tinsel

Our Christmas crib at home, which my father collected and presented to my mother in instalments, may only have had one camel for three wise men but it did have something I haven't seen in any other – a cleaning woman with a broom. Christ was, of course, born in a stable or a cave but that was no reason for it to be filthy. Our crib, like the Christmas story itself, didn't depend on glitter and glamour. It was real.

Sadly, Christmas has lost that reality in a sea of tinsel, trinkets and toys. The way the story is presented now you'd think Mary and Joseph had booked into a four-star hotel with en-suite facilities. In truth, she was a single mother. They were away from home. The baby was due at any moment and they had nowhere to stay. Put yourself in that situation. Would you rush to get out the decorations? I think you'd more likely be frantically searching for the local maternity unit.

Now, as then, Bethlehem can be very bleak at this time of year. It certainly isn't a pretty town, and when people are up to their eyes with work they tend to ignore the stranger, especially the stranger who might make demands. Mary and Joseph were only in Bethlehem because they had to be there for the census. If they'd had their way they would have stayed among friends in Nazareth. For them, that December night was both lonely and stressful. Just as every Christmas will be for many people, especially those who have no one to share it with or who are struggling to find the time and money it demands.

However, Mary and Joseph at least knew that in their difficulties God was with them; that's the meaning of Emmanuel, one of Jesus' names. They were doing what God had called them to do. They realized there was no way to avoid the difficulties and that they had to cope with them, not resent them. Having done so, they not only had a beautiful baby boy but also the whole heavenly host to supply the music and local shepherds with whom to share their joy. Who could ask for more?

Unless we recover the true meaning of Christmas behind the tarnished tinsel there will be a certain hollowness to our celebrations. So, as you celebrate the birth of the Babe of Bethlehem year upon year, look at the reality behind the story rather than at the trappings that disguise it. Then, even into the darkest corners of your life a light will shine, the Light of the World.

Fear not

Running throughout the Christmas story is a command that was obeyed at the time that it was written, but is often forgotten today. The command is 'Fear not', or in modern translations, 'Do not be afraid'.

Zechariah was the first to hear it. He and his wife Elizabeth longed for a child, but she was past child-bearing age. Still, their prayers continued.

Then, one day, when Zechariah was in the temple, he experienced the presence of an angel. 'Fear not,' said the angel, 'for thy prayer is heard; and thy wife Elizabeth shall bear thee a son and thou shalt call his name John.'

Their child became John the Baptist and was the person who fearlessly prepared the way for Jesus.

The second person who was told not to be afraid was Mary. This time it was the Archangel Gabriel who gave the command.

Gabriel told Mary that the Holy Spirit would come upon her and that the power of the Highest would overshadow her, and that 'the child to be born will be called holy, the Son of God.'

Shepherds are not people who are easily frightened, but surrounded by the whole heavenly host, even they started to shake. To them the angel of the Lord said: 'Do not be afraid; for I bring you good news of a great joy, which will come to all the people; for to you is born this day in the city of David a Saviour, who is Christ the Lord.'

Their fear faded and the shepherds immediately made their way to Bethlehem to see this very special baby, who was to show in his own life that the only way fear can be conquered is by love.

For me, the whole Christmas story is summed up in some words from the First Letter of John: 'There is no fear in love, but perfect love casts out fear.' And there can be no greater love than God sending his only Son to be the saviour of the world.

2

Doubts and Fears

As a young curate back in the 1960s I was fearful of expressing any doubts, especially in sermons. So when I prepared a sermon, if I had any lingering doubts, I would put a thick black line in the margin. Then when I came to deliver that sermon the line would catch my eye. It meant 'point weak, shout louder'. In my naïveté I thought that by putting extra force behind the voice I could dispel all doubts in my own mind and any fears in the minds of my listeners. How stupid can you be! People are not fooled by such tricks.

As I have matured in the faith, I have come to realize that from doubt can come strength. Rather like Jacob, I now wrestle with doubts rather than shy away from them, which generally means in the end I understand more than I did. It also means that I can't cope with people who have everything about their faith cut and dried. Jesus Christ may be the same yesterday, today and for ever but like him we are driven by the Spirit. We have to keep our minds open to the developing word and work of God. Closed minds don't make for a vibrant faith.

The person whose name is synonymous with doubt is St Thomas. Not being there on the first Easter night, he missed out on seeing the risen Lord. But at least Thomas had the courage to express his doubts and for that I respect him. As Jesus said, Thomas was fortunate. He had his doubts dispelled by the physical presence of Christ. It is our faith, our minds and our hearts that will help us to overcome our doubts.

Doubt often has a travelling companion: fear. The Christmas story is full of fear. Zechariah was gripped with fear. Mary was greatly troubled. Joseph was told not to be afraid, as were the shepherds. A fear that was overcome by the birth of a baby. Living in fear means living without faith.

St John, in both the Gospel and the first Epistle that bear his name, has some very reassuring words about fear. In the Gospel he quotes Jesus, 'Peace I leave with you; my peace I give you. I do not give to you as the world gives. Do not let your heart be troubled and do not let it be afraid.' And in the first Epistle he writes, 'There is no fear in love. But perfect love drives out fear, because fear has to do with punishment. The one who fears is not made perfect in love.' Actually the one who fears tends to run and hide, as Adam did.

Depths of despair

You can imagine how I felt when on one of my fortnightly visits to Manchester I opened my paper and saw, 'Manchester "least healthy place for men in England"'. I read on only to discover that the third least healthy place is Lambeth, where I live, followed in fifth place by Southwark, which is where I work.

With odds like that against me, what chance have I of survival? Still, as usual, I picked myself up, brushed myself down and started over again.

For some people that wouldn't have been so easy. Bad luck seems to dog their footsteps and clouds are always on the horizon. It's no wonder they feel depressed.

Once depression sets in, life becomes a chore. At least now we realize that depression is an illness, with both physical and mental symptoms, and tablets can bring some relief. But no one wants to become dependent on drugs for the rest of their life. There's no point in saying. 'Pull yourself together!' That only makes matters worse. So how do we cope with feelings of depression in ourselves and others?

Depression comes from feelings of worthlessness and lack of self-esteem. To the outside observer you may look successful, organized and content. But to yourself the picture is very different. Everything you do is an effort and gives you little pleasure or sense of achievement.

For some, even their faith doesn't alleviate the pain or numbness of depression. Just as they feel rejected by other people, they also feel rejected by God.

And yet at the heart of the Christian faith is the importance of the individual. We're told by Jesus we're so valued by God that every hair on our head is numbered. And most important, when Jesus gave his summary of the Commandments he told us that as well as loving other people we should also love ourselves. In the end, that's the only cure for depression.

Persecution complex

I cut myself while shaving and the blood stained my clean collar. My computer went on the blink. I couldn't find my keys and when I got to the Underground station I just missed a train. I then realized that I'd forgotten my clerical vestments. All this and it was a Monday morning. It was just too much. I really thought that God had got it in for me.

I generally work on Sundays – in fact, some people think Sunday is the only day I work – so Monday doesn't have the same sense of dread for me as it does for other people. But I still loathe any day that begins badly. And I'm ashamed to say that when it does, it's God who gets the blame.

How stupid and short-sighted! God didn't make me cut myself. He didn't hide my keys or put a virus in my computer. These things happen: sometimes it's our own fault and at other times nobody's to blame. Certainly not God.

Why do we think God has got it in for us? First of all, when anything goes wrong, the last person we want to blame is ourselves so God becomes a very convenient whipping boy. Second, many of us are riddled with guilt. So the moment things start to go wrong we think it's God getting his own back, that he's seizing the opportunity to punish us and keep us under control.

This is a very primitive reaction. It's superstition rather than faith. People in the past saw God in these terms but I can assure you that sort of God doesn't make any sense to me. God is the ultimate judge but this muddled thinking turns him into someone who is both petty and spiteful. That isn't the God I worship.

Oh, I've just remembered, on that fateful Monday, the bleeper on the cooker wouldn't stop and some mice had made a meal out of my back copies of *Woman's Weekly*. God may not have been against me but I'm not sure who was on my side!

Fearing the worst

Answering-machines are a mixed blessing. They can double your phone bill and your workload. In my experience, there are times when it pays to be unavailable, but I must admit I generally enjoy receiving messages. And the machine works wonders with those idle or forgetful people who claim that they've been trying to call you but you're always out.

However, there are some messages I dread. They begin with the words: 'Hello Roger, it's so-and-so. Could you ring me back as soon as possible?' There's then a click and the line goes dead. I know it's silly but when this happens I always fear the worst.

If it's a personal call, I imagine someone's ill or has died. If it's a business call, I think it's to tell me they're not satisfied with my work or, even worse, that my services are no longer needed.

I know it's irrational and I try to fight it. After all, if you let yourself be dominated by a negative and pessimistic attitude to life, you'll be plagued by unnecessary worry and panic.

There are those who actually prefer to fear the worst, reasoning that if the news is bad, it doesn't come as a shock, and if it's good, there's a blessed sense of relief. But this is no way to run a life. Yes, we must be realistic but that doesn't mean we constantly have to look on the grim side of everything.

Jesus was always straightforward and direct with his disciples. If they were going to face danger, he warned them of it so that they could be prepared. If happiness and joy lay ahead, then he shared that with them too.

None of us can hope for life to be a bowl of cherries all the time, but nor should we expect it to be a vale of tears. By fearing the worst, we often bring suffering on ourselves. How much better it is to keep an open mind. Then, when we do get the news, we can either rejoice or summon the courage to cope. And, what's more, we'll be at full strength as we won't have wasted any of it on unnecessary anxious anticipation.

Digging the dirt

After reading the Sunday papers it isn't just my hands I need to wash, my mind needs a good scrub too! I don't know about you, but after about an hour with the papers, tabloid and broadsheet, I feel grubby. It seems as though we have an insatiable appetite for news about the weaknesses of others, especially if they're famous. The break-up of a pop star's marriage can take precedence over war, famine and disease. An illicit sexual affair between two prominent people can supplant international news. Even rumour and gossip are often preferred to fact. If they get it wrong, the papers usually apologize but, more often than not, the apology is nowhere near as prominent as the original story. And besides, by then the damage is likely to have been done.

Newspapers always claim they wouldn't publish the stories if the public didn't want them or if they didn't sell papers. Although I don't believe this is the whole truth – after all, it's quite possible to create a demand rather than just satisfy one – in the main I think they're right. We do love to hear about other people's sins and misfortunes, no matter what pain it causes those concerned. But why is this?

What's often at the heart of this is self-righteousness. While mud is being thrown at other people we can feel smug ourselves. As the Bible puts it, while we concentrate on the speck in another's eye, we may have a plank in our own. This isn't the only teaching that Jesus gave about self-righteousness. 'Judge not that you be not judged' is a very good motto to have in mind when you're reading about and maybe enjoying the failings of others. This theme is continued in St John's Gospel when Jesus comes across a crowd stoning a woman who had been caught in the act of adultery. 'Let he who is without sin cast the first stone,' says Jesus, and within seconds the crowd has disappeared. And although Jesus doesn't condemn the woman, he does tell her to 'go and sin no more'.

In contrast, we are nearly always ready to condemn, whether we know the whole story or not. So the next time you take delight, or even an interest, in someone else's misfortune, ask yourself what that says about you. Are you truly concerned about them or are you just gloating?

Leathal cocktail

I recently visited Versailles, outside Paris, and discovered that, like many palaces, it has a tale or two to tell. Built originally as a hunting lodge, it was transformed into one of the greatest palaces in Europe by the Sun King, Louis XIV. Although hunting continued, Louis' main sport seems to have centred on women rather than animals.

One of his favourites was Madame de Montespan, whom he met at a supper where there were more than 300 women present. An affair started. Things became complicated when it was discovered that she was pregnant and the king was the father. She did her best to conceal the pregnancy while at the same time planning with the king to find a woman that would take the infant at birth and look after it secretly. Madame de Montespan knew just the right person – Madame Scarron, a pretty young widow of noble birth who had fallen on hard times and was lodging in a Paris convent. Faced with this dilemma, Madame Scarron consulted her confessor, while Madame de Montespan was far more likely to see her fortune-teller.

Deciding whom you should turn to at a time of crisis is never easy. However, if it comes to a choice between a fortune-teller and a confessor there's no competition. The confessor would win hands down. Some people, of course, would hedge their bets and consult both. But when the world of faith gets muddled with the world of superstition we're heading for trouble. Superstition will always imprison you. Think of those people whose day is brought to an absolute standstill on every Friday the 13th. The fear is totally irrational but, because it's a mixture of religion and superstition, it has a powerful effect. Friday was the day on which Jesus was crucified and 13 people sat down to the Last Supper. So Friday the 13th has become a date to be feared.

Thirteen is such a dreaded number that some blocks of flats have no 13th floor, there's no row 13 on aircraft and some streets miss out number 13. Even some who call themselves believers still allow superstition to have a hold over them. While saying that they believe in God, they let their lives be controlled by numbers, magpies, ladders and black cats.

True religion brings freedom. It allows people to be themselves and to give of their best. You certainly won't feel free if you let your life be controlled by superstition. Mixing superstition with religion only produces a highly dangerous cocktail.

The pain of guilt

I'm always sad when I receive a letter that's unsigned and has no address. Especially if it comes from someone in need. Obviously I can remember the situation in my prayers but in many cases I would like to do more than that.

This particular letter came from a woman who was riddled with guilt. Years ago she had trained as a nurse. Often the wards she was on were short staffed and she felt that she couldn't always get the help, support and advice she needed. Now, instead of remembering those days with happiness and a sense of achievement, she remembers them solely with guilt. Her mind flashes with the possible fear that she might have given someone the wrong drug or an incorrect dose. 'What if someone died or was damaged by my mistake?'; that's the cancerous thought that eats into her soul.

As far as I know there is no evidence that anyone did suffer as a result of her inexperience. I should think that most people were very grateful for her attentive care. But that means nothing to my letter-writer. It's the guilt of what *might* have happened that haunts her.

This sort of guilt is destructive and ill-placed. We can never be guilty of things that we didn't do, though we can be guilty of not doing things we know to be right. We cannot be spiritually guilty of things that through lack of experience or understanding we have done. We are only guilty of acts or thoughts that we know are wrong.

Although many people do, there is no point in torturing yourself unnecessarily. Guilt is only beneficial when it encourages you to ask for forgiveness both from God and those you've hurt. Guilt is positive where it teaches you to change your ways. It isn't a stick to beat yourself with. It's a reminder that you can do better and it's only effective when you've actually done something wrong in the first place.

Firing on all cylinders

It doesn't matter whether it's the press, the Church or politicians, the question is still the same. Who or what are you to believe? Newspapers often produce totally conflicting reports of the same event. Different Christian churches put differing emphasis on various beliefs. Politicians say one thing while in opposition and do the opposite when in power. Who or what are you to believe?

Faced with such confusion many people just give up, adopting the attitude 'a plague on all your houses'. Yet as humans we have a need to believe, otherwise our lives only fire on one cylinder. There's a dimension of our lives missing.

All belief involves trust. This was Thomas' problem. He wasn't prepared to trust either the women who'd been to the empty tomb or the disciples who'd seen Jesus the previous week. Rather than trust, he wanted proof. While Moses was away talking with God, Aaron, encouraged by the Children of Israel, decided to build the golden calf. After all, there was the vague possibility that Moses wouldn't return, so they decided to hedge their bets. Just in case Yahweh proved untrustworthy, they thought they'd get alongside another god.

Without a trusting belief our lives just drift. It was much easier when everything was either right or wrong. You obviously believed what was right and did your best to forsake what was wrong. Now, with our greater understanding, we're faced with decisions that the people of biblical times never had to face. For them, belief still involved trust. It was just that belief then was much more straightforward.

'I believe, help thou my unbelief' was the heartfelt plea of the father of the young boy with epilepsy. He knew he needed to believe but, like many of us, he found belief difficult. However, he also realized that without belief, even if he had occasional doubts, his son wouldn't be healed.

Doubts will never totally disappear but they can be coped with when faced by a foundation of faith.

Making the right choice

It used to be so simple. There was only one gas company, one electricity company and one telephone company. The only decision you had to make was 'take it or leave it'. But now ... !

I don't know whether I'm coming or going. You tell me whether it would be cheaper to have gas from an electricity company or electricity from a gas company. And I still haven't a clue if I'm getting the best deal for my telephone.

It's all very complicated. But then choice always is. Our family background is bound to affect the way we make our initial choices, but sooner or later the choices we make must be our own responsibility. It's then that life becomes difficult.

The pressures on young people are greater than they have ever been. From the word go they're faced with choice. From the moment they can influence their parents on which breakfast cereal they have, the advertisers won't leave them alone. Peer group pressure forces youngsters to make choices many wouldn't have dreamed of on their own. But as adults, the choice must be ours.

In the Sermon on the Mount, Jesus has some straightforward and very demanding words to say about choices. He's already hammered his audience with the knowledge that the thought is as bad as the deed. He's rebuked them over their lack of faith and their judgmental attitude. But before he ends, he has a few well-chosen words to say about the choices we make in life.

'Enter by the narrow gate; for the gate is wide and the way is easy, that leads to destruction, and those who enter by it are many. For the gate is narrow and the way is hard, that leads to life, and those who find it are few.'

Choosing whether to take the narrow or the wide gate isn't, I believe, a once-and-for-all choice. It needs to be made daily. The wide gate will always be the more immediately attractive. But choices should bear in mind the long-term future rather than the short-term gains.

A good argument

Some people have firm opinions and are not shy about sharing them with the world. Do you ever read the 'celebrity' columnists in newspapers? Sometimes it seems they issue their outpourings on ignorance, misinformation and prejudice, and certainly they don't let doubt or fairness get in the way of a good story. After all, controversy sells papers.

Most of us enjoy a good argument. Life would be very dull if we all agreed on everything, and a little lively debate keeps us interested and alert. Jesus seemed to thrive on it. Some of the statements he made were highly controversial and he never shied away from a good argument.

He didn't hesitate to tackle such sensitive topics as healing on the Sabbath Day, the treatment of an adulterous woman and the payment of taxes. He had very definite views on these and many other subjects and the fact that these were at odds with those of the religious leaders of his time didn't bother him one bit. He would take on anyone.

The Christian Church has never turned away from controversy either. Nor should it. Birth control, euthanasia, homosexuality, divorce, world debt and abortion are subjects on which it should not be afraid to voice its views.

However, since the Church is an organization made up of human beings, it's often unable to speak with a single, clear voice. Fewer people are able to accept *ex cathedra* statements from on high these days. Many people are also unwilling to take the words 'The Bible says' as an end to all argument. After all, the Bible says many things on many subjects and not all its views are acceptable today.

Just as Jesus made the people of his time rethink their values, so I believe the Holy Spirit encourages us to do the same. The foundation of Christian belief will always be to love God and love our neighbour as ourselves, but how we apply this is bound to differ from the approach of people 2,000 or even 200 years ago. Global markets, hi-tech communications, deeper medical and psychological understanding must colour our thinking.

Christians who act as though everything is cut and dried are far less challenging than controversial ones.

Keep it open

As I was reading a small book called *Spiritual Pain*, this sentence hit me right between the eyes: 'We have to remember that our hearts and minds are like a parachute, they only really work when they are open.' I put down the book, plugged in my computer and started writing this.

The openness of a parachute is something we can all envisage. The closure of minds and hearts is something we all experience, in ourselves or other people.

A closed mind leads to bigotry, a closed heart to loneliness, and yet we still believe they provide some sort of protection. Well, I suppose in a way they do. An open mind means we constantly have to rethink our attitudes and opinions. An open heart means that we're vulnerable. Others may take advantage. But do we really want this kind of protection?

Jesus was a constant campaigner against closed minds and hearts. It was because people lived in their self-contained worlds that they failed to understand who he was or what he was about. He challenged them to think again. He criticized his disciples because at times their minds were closed. He wanted everyone to be honest and open, even if it meant hearing things that were hard to take. Peter certainly didn't want to hear that Jesus was destined to die. He said so and he was rebuked: 'Get behind me, Satan. You think as men think, not as God thinks.'

Openness is neither a soft nor an easy option, but unless we're prepared to be open we will remain isolated. Then we will wonder why our lives are empty.

Openness has nothing to do with age. I've met elderly people who have wonderfully open hearts and minds: my aunt, who's in her 90s, is one of them. I've also met young and middle-aged people who are amazingly bigoted.

Having an open mind doesn't mean you agree with everyone, with no mind of your own. But it does mean you're prepared to listen and discuss. Having an open heart means you're able to trust, and that's vital in any relationship.

Something new?

New religious movements and cults have come into their own as people have turned away from conventional religion. Not just the young, but people of all ages are looking for something that makes spiritual sense to them, and some are turning elsewhere for spiritual satisfaction.

I believe that all cults should carry a spiritual as well as a physical health warning. It's not easy to define what a cult is, but ever since 1978, when a community of more than 900 people in Jonestown, Guyana, died in a mass suicide, the word cult has referred to both religious and non-religious groups where coercion and harm are clearly taking place. Many people are drawn into cults when they are at their lowest ebb. Someone shows them kindness and, before they know it, their lives are no longer their own. Often brainwashed, they are turned against friends and family. Worldly possessions are held in common and total commitment is demanded.

The term 'new religious movement' is used to cover a wide variety of religious groups, some of which can be found within as well as outside established traditions. Not all these groups will claim to be religious, but many will have a charismatic leader and will claim to offer the answer to life. Again these groups demand commitment and loyalty. They also expect contributions in money, property, time and work. Nor are they easy to leave.

The search for spiritual strength is never easy. Many people feel let down or ignored by traditional churches and so I am not really surprised when they sometimes look elsewhere. But I believe they're often looking for the wrong thing. All of us would like answers to the deep questions of life but we're not meant to have them handed to us on a plate.

Belief in God asks as many questions as it gives answers. Religion lays down certain rules and guidelines but it *doesn't* remove either our free will or our responsibility to think for ourselves. If we resort to either quick fixes or easy answers, our spiritual satisfaction will be short-lived. It's only when we're prepared to live with questions, face difficulties and overcome doubt that we will have a faith that is both meaningful and lasting.

Spirit of triumph

Most of the party invitations I receive are from people celebrating their 50th, 60th or even 90th birthdays. So to be invited to a 21st was a real treat. I knew the music would be far too loud and there would be very little chance of a fox-trot, but who cared? It's great when the young don't think you're past your sell-by date and aren't embarrassed by your company. Donning my dinner jacket, I set off for what turned out to be a really fantastic evening.

I've known Svend for seven years from when, due to his physical disabilities, he was a student at Lord Mayor Treloar College. Svend may be physically restricted in a wheelchair, but his mind is as active as any mind can be. His sense of humour is wicked and his thoughtfulness for others knows no bounds.

In proposing a toast to him, his godfather remarked how one word kept coming back to him as he wrote his speech: triumph. In his reply, Svend proved how apt that word was. He doesn't find speaking terribly easy but he had prepared and repeatedly rehearsed a speech that he was determined to deliver, and deliver it he did, in excellent style. He thanked his mother for the tremendous support she had given him and presented her with a marvellous bouquet of flowers. He paid tribute to his father who had died eight years before and whose last words to Svend were that everything would be all right. He also thanked his two brothers for being 'the best in the world'. The attention paid to the speech and the applause at the end were amazing. Once again, Svend had triumphed.

I had got to know Svend well when he was in hospital following complications after major surgery. Like anyone else, he experienced times when he felt fed up but, as usual, he adopted the attitude that it was something to be overcome. And so he did. Another triumph.

When life is difficult, it's all too easy to give in. Had Jesus succumbed to the temptations in the wilderness, the pressure in the Garden of Gethsemane or the taunts when he was on the Cross, he would not have fulfilled his Father's will. He worked through and overcame these trials by prayer, by determination and by the support of others. He triumphed. And so can we. When hardships come, don't give in. Get help. For it is by prayer, friendship and courage that difficulties can be overcome and disasters turned to triumphs.

3

Hopes and Joys

For the Promenader, Britain is the Land of Hope and Glory. 'All hope abandon, ye who enter here' is the grim instruction given by Dante in his *Divine Comedy* to those who are about to enter hell. But then hell is without hope whereas for heaven and earth it is the life-blood.

The moment hope goes from a person's life they are as good as dead, spiritually and emotionally, if not physically. That is why I find hospices are oases of hope in what could often be regarded as a hopeless situation. In their treatment of patients as whole people, people who are made up of body, mind and spirit, hospice staff make sure that their patients are never without hope. They are also aware that patients have families and friends, and if they are to be of support during this vital stage in a person's life then they too must have hope. Not false hope, but realistic hope. They need to believe that from suffering can come joy, from death can come life. One of the hardest things that Jesus had to tell his disciples was how he was going to die. Impetuous Peter couldn't take it, said so, and earned from Jesus one of the stiffest rebukes in the Gospels.

However, if he had listened carefully Peter would have heard that even that stark statement was not without hope. 'In three days I shall rise from the dead' was the message of hope. It was the fulfilment of that hopeful promise on the first Easter Day that freed Peter and the others from the imprisonment of the Upper Room and gave them the strength to preach Christ crucified.

Hope automatically acts as a springboard for joy. There is nothing more wonderful than the face of a young child when a dream comes true and a hope has been fulfilled. It can often be something quite simple, like catching sight of someone they love. Suddenly their face radiates joy, a joy that is highly infectious. I have only to hear a child chuckle and happiness fills my heart. Sadly, as we grow older we become more cynical. We look for hidden motives. We are not prepared to trust. We prefer to argue the case. We become half-hearted about hope and lacklustre about joy. If that is the case then it is no wonder that Jesus said, 'Unless you become like little children you shall in no way enter the Kingdom of Heaven', as two of the main ingredients of that kingdom are hope and joy.

Hope from despair

It isn't often I quote directly from a letter, but this one is rather special. It came from Jan in Leicester. 'It was the fourth year I'd been alone since my husband Barrie had died on Christmas Day,' she wrote. 'A car knocked him down three days before, when he was coming home after Christmas shopping, causing him severe brain damage. I'd turned on the radio just as you were telling the audience about a young lady that wanted a piece of music because four years before somebody had donated her an organ for transplant.'

According to Jan, I went on to say how much I respected both those who made organ donations and those who allowed their loved ones' organs to be donated. Despite her sadness, Jan and her two sons had the comfort of knowing that Barrie's death had not been totally in vain. Some good had come out of their tragedy.

Gifts of new life were given to seven people in England and Europe. Barrie's heart had been given to a man with five children. His liver was given to a young woman who could then have a child. Jan ended her letter by saying, 'Christmas now has its true meaning of gifts from God. Thank you, Roger, for another lesson straight from God directed through you for me. That's love.'

That letter was one of the most moving I've ever read. It taught me that you never know how the things you say may influence other people, although I realize that I'm very privileged as a broadcaster to be able to say things that I hope will help many people. But all of us who have the power of speech are able to influence others.

I also realized that Jan was in fact experiencing the message of Jesus' life: joy from sadness, hope from despair. It's good to remember that in the face of even the greatest tragedy.

Beacon of light

Before her death the world-famous novelist Iris Murdoch's life had descended into the darkness of Alzheimer's disease, the destructive illness that ruins the lives of many and makes untold demands on those who love and care for them. A woman whose whole life had been words now found it difficult both to speak coherently and to understand.

In this darkness there was one beacon of light – her husband John Bayley. A writer himself, he put his thoughts into a book called *Iris: A Memoir of Iris Murdoch*. As I read it, tears filled my eyes. They were tears of sadness but also of joy, respect and admiration.

One time, a woman whose husband suffered from Alzheimer's said to John, 'It's like being chained to a corpse, isn't it?' Adding, 'A much loved corpse, naturally.' He realized that she was trying to be understanding, but she'd got it wrong.

For John, there was frustration and anger, but also the quiet, private moments of shared joy, love and humour. He couldn't always be sure that Iris understood the situation, but by her smile, at least, she appeared to.

All certainly was not darkness. There was light and the light was love. It was that love which gave life. Iris was certainly not a conventional religious believer, but she was a deeply spiritual person. In the way that John cared for her, I can see the whole theme of death and resurrection hope overcoming despair and joy dominating sadness.

Although they may not have seen it as such, here was Christian faith in action, a reminder that even in our darkest times there is light.

For a believer, darkness must never be allowed to dominate. My hope is that John is now receiving, from those who love him, the care that he so willingly gave to Iris.

Body and soul

Some surveys leave me cold. I need neither surveys nor experts to tell me that a little bit of dirt doesn't hurt children and that it can often build up resistance to disease. However, I was interested in another survey that maintained that people with religious beliefs lived longer and, on the whole, were healthier. Whether it's true or not, I don't know, but it certainly made me think.

Some religious beliefs ought to carry a health warning, as they're both dangerous and subversive. But true faith does make a firm foundation for life. Faith in God helps you realize that you are part of his creation and, as such, you have a part to play. You're not on your own. You're not a self-made man or woman, and the gifts that you have come from God.

That's why when Jesus is asked to name the chief commandment, he begins by saying, 'You shall love the Lord your God with all your heart, and with all your soul, and with all your strength, and with all your mind.' He does, however, go on from there: 'You shall love your neighbour.'

Those at peace with their neighbours are bound to be in a better state of mind than those who are constantly at war. People who look for the good in others have a far less stressful life than those who constantly criticize others. They'll be let down from time to time, but at least their overall attitude to other people is positive.

There's also a third part to Jesus' summary of the Law. As well as loving God and your neighbour, Jesus also tells us to love ourselves. There can be nothing healthier than having a proper love of oneself. We're not talking here about arrogance. We're talking about being aware of our weaknesses, knowing our strengths and realizing that we are of value. The sense of belonging that true faith can give us certainly gives strength to our souls. And when the soul is in good heart, the body generally benefits.

Nobody's perfect

The inclusion of 'if only' or 'but' in a sentence is a sure-fire way of degrading something or someone. 'If only the photographer hadn't taken so long with the photos, it would have been a lovely wedding.' What was otherwise a very happy occasion is remembered mainly because a photographer took a while to make sure that he got the photos the couple wanted. Forget the beautiful service, delicious food and plentiful drink, that wedding will always be remembered for the long wait. 'Have you met Louise? She's a really nice woman and does a tremendous amount for charity.'

'Yes, but did you know she left her first husband after 18 years of marriage?'

Some people appear to be incapable of hearing anything nice about anyone without adding 'Yes, but . . .'. It's so sad.

All of us have a side we'd prefer to keep hidden. Nobody's perfect, but the vast majority of us are predominantly good rather than evil. So, how much better it is to look on the good side than to dwell on the faults.

Jesus seemed to have the knack of doing that. Mary Magdalene, Matthew, even Peter, could all be categorized as 'Yes, but . . .' people. All had weaknesses to their characters and yet Jesus was able to spot their strengths.

The Dutch teenager Anne Frank must be one of the greatest examples this century of a person who lived by this philosophy.

Despite being imprisoned in a cramped Amsterdam annexe and eventually dying in Belsen, she was able to write this in her diary: 'It's a wonder I haven't abandoned all my ideals, they seem so absurd and impractical. Yet I cling to them because I still believe, in spite of everything, that people are truly good at heart. It is utterly impossible for me to build my life on a foundation of chaos, suffering and death . . . I feel the suffering of millions. And yet when I look up at the sky I somehow feel everything will change for the better.'

No 'ifs' or 'buts' there.

All things bright and beautiful

All hell was let loose when the Bishop of Leeds had the nerve to attack Mrs Alexander's much-loved hymn, *All Things Bright and Beautiful*. What really annoyed him was the verse about the rich man in his castle, the poor man at his gate. According to the hymn, not only was this situation acceptable, it was actually ordered by God.

This wasn't actually what Mrs Alexander had meant. She wanted to show that God loved everyone, whatever their situation. However, the bishop was a brave man to make such an outspoken comment on such a popular hymn. After more than five years of presenting BBC Radio 2's hymn-singing programme *Sunday Half Hour*, I've learnt that hymns are precious to many.

And so are their tunes. You have what some regard as 'the wrong tune' to their favourite hymn and, take it from me, the vitriolic letters come flying. In reply to one correspondent, I dared to say I thought there was no such thing as 'the right tune', and that opened a real can of worms.

In many school assemblies now hymns are rarely sung. But I still remember school halls, conscripted choirs, fraught music teachers and half-hearted hymn-singing – half-hearted that is until we caught the headteacher's eye. Then we sang for all we were worth.

Hymns have associations with special occasions and so become very precious. People remember the ones they sang at their wedding or at a loved one's funeral. I can't imagine Wembley without *Abide With Me* or Cardiff Arms Park without *Cwm Rhondda* – it would be a shame if hymn-singing was restricted to church services.

Many people have their understanding of God from hymns. The message may be misleading or even inaccurate, but at least hymns provide a user-friendly basis from which religious thoughts can develop.

Care with new creation

The cartoonists had an absolute field day. Great-grandmas were pictured coming out of maternity wards and children were seen discussing the respective ages of their parents. Certainly they weren't short of material with the latest news from the labs, that the menopause can be reversed and fertility put on hold.

Obviously I must be careful here, as I am a man talking about a woman's world, but I do think that there's a spiritual side to this scientific discovery.

Now, I'm not a fundamentalist. I fully accept that ideas, and even beliefs, can change. When you think that at one time certain Christians believed both slavery and apartheid were not only acceptable, but also the will of God, you'll realize that some changes can't come soon enough. However, when we're talking about new lives, a new creation, a new eternal soul, I don't think we can be too careful.

I have three very good friends who were unable to have children of their own because of infertility. It caused them enormous pain. But I think there are times when we have to take a closer look at the long-term effects of our new-found knowledge. Both my parents were regarded as quite elderly when I was born, and sadly both were dead before I left school. Medical care has improved greatly since those days, but I can assure you it's no fun losing both your parents at an early age.

We're also not exactly short of people in this world. We're not that good at getting on together, and many people are living in conditions that are totally unacceptable. Although a lot of people may see this development as a ray of hope, I pray that it isn't a false hope, and that we haven't gained for ourselves another scientific success without taking into account all its social, spiritual and personal implications.

A midsummer night's dream

I can't ever remember having a dream on midsummer night; well certainly not one that would rival Shakespeare's magnificent spectacular. But I have been involved in midsummer madness. When I was living in the West Country, some friends suggested that we get up at some ridiculous hour to greet the midsummer dawn on one of the hills associated with King Arthur's Camelot. It was a pleasant enough experience; but the event was underpinned by champagne, so that may have helped.

Romping around a Somerset hill on midsummer morning with a glass in my hand made me feel quite pagan. Yet it was also a deeply religious experience, a chance to appreciate with others the beauty of God's creation.

Pagan people of yesteryear knew they were dependent on creation. They treated it with great respect, knowing both its beauty and its power. You mucked around with creation at your own peril.

Today we take creation for granted; we certainly think we can control it. What we've forgotten is that creation is a continuing process. We're surprised by earthquakes and volcanoes. We destroy the rainforests or part of the earth's atmosphere and then we wonder why climatic conditions have changed. We alter the course of a river and can't understand why there are floods.

Humankind is the most sophisticated part of creation but this doesn't give us *carte blanche* to do what we want. To me, as there is a creation so there must be a Creator. This doesn't mean I think everything happened in six days and God put his feet up on the seventh. It means, I believe, every living thing was created for a purpose. Finding out what that purpose is isn't always easy, but we'll never find it if we're selfish or destructive.

It might help if we treated creation with awe and wonder; it's an old-fashioned idea but a good one. If we occasionally took some time to consider the world in which we live, we might realize what a wonderful place it is. We might even find ourselves having a midsummer night's dream or enjoying a touch of midsummer madness.

Come rain or shine

Until she moved earlier in the year, Babs was, without fail, at the 8 a.m. Holy Communion service at my local church. She was in her 70s and had been attending St Anselm's for a lot longer than me. Come rain or shine, hail, sleet or snow, Babs was sitting in her seat at the far left-hand corner of the front row. Even when she could no longer drive her car and had quite a way to walk, Babs never missed. Her health wasn't that good and her life wasn't easy, but somehow she always made sure that each new week began with that service.

She wouldn't describe herself as a pious person. Nor was she naïve. There were times when she thought that God had dealt her a difficult hand. But she knew that, unless her week began with the worship of God, there was something missing in her life.

Loyalty, faithfulness and commitment were the three guiding factors in Babs' life, whereas they seem to be missing from many people's lives. It could be a generation thing, but I really don't think so. Faithfulness and loyalty are not valued in the way that they were.

Material objects are not made to last. More and more things are disposable. And what's true of things is certainly true of people. Very few of today's youngsters will stay in the same job for the whole of their lives. This may well be a good thing but it also creates uncertainty and it doesn't instil loyalty.

Employers don't think twice about getting rid of some of their most experienced staff the moment profit margins begin to slide, and employees only stay with a job as long as it suits them. And if that's true about work, it's also true about marriage. The increasing divorce rate in this country shows that loyalty and faithfulness are things of the past. Faithfulness is highly commended by Christ. He points out, 'He who is faithful in a very little is also faithful in much.' So it's not surprising that it's the 'good and faithful' servant who's rewarded.

Scents of occasion

I promise you that I haven't been rummaging around in his bathroom, but when I discovered that I use the same aftershave as the Prime Minister, I didn't know whether to be flattered or embarrassed.

The newspapers that revealed the Prime Minister's grooming habits seemed more concerned with its price than its smell. This brand certainly isn't cheap but, if Tony Blair has any sense, he'll do as I do and purchase as much as he can in the duty-free lounge before he flies off to some summit or other.

I'd never heard of this particular aftershave until I was given a bottle as a Christmas present by a most discerning gentleman who, at the time, was editor of a woman's magazine. Until then I hadn't been faithful to one brand, since most of my aftershaves had been presents. Some took my skin off, some attracted the flies but at least I felt better prepared to face the outside world.

Smell is important and the aftershave the Prime Minister and I use has a pleasant fragrance. It isn't too heavy. It isn't too sickly. And though it's too extravagant to splash all over, used sparingly it can make you feel really good.

The sense of smell is God-given and those deprived of it, though perhaps not suffering as much as those who have lost their sight or hearing, are missing one of the riches of life. They may be protected from odious odours but they're unable to share in the delightful aroma of bread baking, coffee percolating or new-mown grass.

At one garden festival I attended there was a section set aside for blind people. Its strength was in its scent. As I walked around, with my eyes shut, I realized how much I miss in life by concentrating on sight and ignoring smell. It seems utterly ridiculous that the flowers in some shops should be marked as 'scented'. It has only been our greed and demands to have every flower the whole year through that has meant we now get blooms that may look beautiful and last longer but are missing something vital, their scent.

Both the frankincense and the myrrh given to Jesus at his birth were known for their scent. And smell has always played an important part in Christian worship, as it has in the worship of other faiths. For when we worship God we should worship him with everything that we have, every gift that he has bestowed on us, and that includes our precious sense of smell.

Not what they seem

If there was one group of people Jesus loathed, it was hypocrites, those who pretend to be what they're not or pretend to believe what they don't. In other words, people who don't practise what they preach. He had no time for them at all – unless, of course, they changed their ways.

One of the most common accusations levelled against churchgoers is that they're hypocrites, that they adopt one behaviour for church and another for the rest of their life. And as a clergyman, I have to be constantly on my guard against such accusations, especially if they're justified.

There are occasions when I fail, but a prayer I often use, especially after having taken a church service, is a timely reminder that I should always be aware of the problem. It goes, 'Grant, O Lord, that what we have said and sung with our lips we believe in our hearts, and what we believe in our hearts we show forth in our lives, through Jesus Christ Our Lord, Amen.'

It's very difficult to deal with hypocrites. For example, I was cross when I read that a certain celebrity was a non-believer, even though he'd turned up and sung along in a *Songs of Praise* TV programme I was presenting. To me, that's hypocrisy. If you don't believe, you shouldn't appear on a religious show singing hymns, however much you enjoy the tunes or want to be seen on TV.

Most hypocrites are seen through sooner or later. It becomes harder and harder for them to keep up the pretence. But why be a hypocrite in the first place? Why pretend to be someone you're not? It's incredibly exhausting.

Far better to be the real you. That's the person God loves. The genuine you is far more interesting than the hypocritical you.

Heavenly music

Right now as I write, one of my favourite pieces of music is playing in the background. It never fails to put me in a good mood. It's not Bassey or Cliff. It's a setting for the Christmas Midnight Mass written by the 17th-century French composer Charpentier. Now that may sound rather highbrow but it's not. One music critic said of it, 'Nowhere else in the whole of French Baroque music is there a work of quite such charm; the skill with which Charpentier uses the old French carols as the basis for his composition is remarkable, yet the entire work has a lightness and gentleness completely in keeping with the feast it celebrates.'

I was introduced to this piece of music by a colleague who became a friend.

At a time when I was living in a house that went with my job, I decided, for security's sake, to buy myself a little cottage in Sherborne, Dorset. It was two up, two down and I shared a small courtyard with three very nice neighbours. The thick, stone walls made it extremely cosy, especially in winter when I had a great log fire burning. It was a lovely place to invite people to stay.

One of my fairly regular visitors was Stephen, for whom I later stood as Best Man. Stephen is musical and whenever we went out for a walk and visited local churches, he would play any musical instrument that came to hand. Often it was a harmonium long past its prime. And the tune he always played was the first part of Charpentier's Mass. I grew to love it so much that it was one of the first CDs I ever bought.

Sadly, when I needed to buy a house in London, the cottage had to go. But whenever I listen to this record it isn't just the music I enjoy, it's the memories that accompany it: the glorious Dorset countryside, those wonderful walks and a friendship that has lasted more than 20 years.

Music is very powerful. The hymns you learnt as a child, the tune playing when you met the love of your life, the music that comforted you at a time of great distress still have an important part to play in your life.

It's no wonder music has such a significant place in worship. Music transports us to a higher plane and feeds the spirit in a way beyond mere words.

Cheerful giving

Hardly a day goes by that I don't receive a begging letter from one charity or another. Raising money isn't an easy job, even for the most worthwhile cause, and so charities have to seize every opportunity. But I do feel that some overstep the mark.

Recently I received a letter from a charity I'd never heard of. Enclosed were two penny coins. The letter suggested that if I added my donation to the money they had sent me, wonderful things could be achieved. I don't doubt the sincerity or the value of their appeal, but I object very strongly to the way they set about raising the money. It's a form of blackmail. When a charity gives you money and then asks you to add to it, you're trapped. I decided to put the two pennies in a collecting box and tear up the letter.

Nor was I too pleased when another charity sent me a couple of books of raffle tickets. Again, I hadn't asked for them, they just arrived in the post. This sort of pressure is unfair.

In St Paul's letter to the people of Corinth, he first of all congratulates them on their generosity, which he describes as an example to others. But as always, he needs more help, so he warns them he'll soon be on his way to collect their next generous donation and he'd be grateful if it could be ready for him when he arrives. However, he does make one very important point. The money's to be given willingly and not extracted as an enforced payment. Paul goes on to say, 'The point is this: he who sows sparingly will reap sparingly, and he who sows bountifully will also reap bountifully. Each one must do as he has made up his mind, not reluctantly or under compulsion, for God loves a cheerful giver.'

So I don't think anyone should feel at all guilty about refusing to give to a charity that uses blackmail, or if there's a worry that the money won't be well spent. But when we do give, we should do so generously and with good grace. That's what makes a 'cheerful giver'.

4

Difficulties and Dangers

For some people, they are a challenge. For others, they are a nightmare. I must admit I tend to come into the second category. Difficulties and dangers drag me down. But they shouldn't. They are there either to be overcome or to come to terms with. They are not there to ruin your life.

Thrills and spills have never been part of my life. I wasn't too good on my tiny tricycle. Downhill it went too fast. Uphill it was too much effort. It was a while before I took to two wheels and I was in no hurry to learn to drive. It was the gentler rides I liked at fun fairs.

However, there are times when danger has to be faced. Difficulties must be overcome. To pretend they are not there is to live in a fantasy world with your head in the sand. Danger needs to be faced. Certainly Moses wasn't afraid to face it. Surrounded by the whinging Children of Israel, pursued by the mighty force of the Egyptians and only minutes away from the Red Sea, Moses put his trust in the Lord with miraculous results. Elijah, loathed by Jezebel, seizes a difficult and dangerous situation by the horns and proves that his God is more powerful than Baal. But difficulties and dangers got even Elijah down at times.

One of the problems with difficulties and dangers is that they arrive at the most unexpected times. With ample warning doubtless you would be able to cope. But sadly that is not the nature of the beast. Catching people unaware is the strongest weapon in its armoury.

It means that rather like members of the Baden-Powell movement we have to 'Be Prepared', so that, come what may, we can cope.

Preparation means building your life on a bedrock of prayer because prayer more than anything affects your attitude to life. It gives you a realistic, positive frame of mind that enables you to overcome the dangers and difficulties that cross your path. The Red Sea may not part but you will be more than able to see the light at the end of the tunnel. Difficulties can often be put in your path by people you loathe or who loathe you. Here again prayer can help. Following Jesus' advice in the Sermon on the Mount, you pray for your enemies, not so as to heap burning coals on their heads but to understand them and hopefully diffuse any danger.

True grit

Diamonds may be a girl's best friend but I've never known a woman turn down a string of pearls. They don't have to be teamed with the traditional twin set. Worn against an elegant black dress they can look absolutely stunning.

However, I'm not here to give you fashion hints. I'm more concerned with the contents of your life than its adornments. As you know, it's the grit in the oyster that makes the pearl. Something that starts as an irritant develops into a thing of great beauty. And there's a lesson for us all.

I've always found that it's the people who've struggled with life, who've not given in to their problems and difficulties, who have become the pearls, the ones who really shine and glow. Those for whom life has been easy are often insensitive to the difficulties others face. They've only had to click their fingers for things to happen and they can't understand why it isn't the same for everyone. But it isn't.

It takes time to turn grit into a pearl. It also takes perseverance and a sense of hope. Without these qualities, instead of developing into a pearl, the grit becomes a boulder that blights life rather than beautifies it.

St Paul complained about 'a thorn in the flesh'. Doubtless that grit was the driving force behind his missionary journeys. It was the grit in Moses' life that made him such a wonderful leader for the Children of Israel. It was the grit of Linda McCartney's cancer that made her so aware of the suffering in others. It was the grit in Jesus' life that enabled him to come through the suffering of the Cross to the joy of the Resurrection.

So don't let those difficulties that beset all of us get you down. Turn them into opportunities. Then you can transform the grit in your life into pearls beyond price.

Dirty washing

A few years ago the last of Liverpool's public wash-houses closed. One 84-year-old lady had been using it since she was 17. Another used it every week even though she had her own washing machine at home. They were naturally upset, for no longer would they be able to meet up and have a good gossip. It was the fellowship that they'd really miss.

However, washing your dirty linen in public isn't everybody's idea of fun, especially if the washing is made up of your sins rather than your smalls.

In the early church it was common for confession to be held in public. People didn't enjoy the privacy of a confessional box in the corner of the church, with a priest who was partially hidden. No, they had to tell the whole community exactly what they'd been up to and ask for its prayers and for God's forgiveness. I suppose it was much like a religious group therapy session.

You were expected to expose yourself in public because, in sinning, not only had you let down God, but you'd also let down your fellow Christians. Then, having shared your sins and failures with your fellow believers, you could rely on them for support as you tried to change your ways.

One reason why people are so hesitant to share their failures is that they're frightened they will be held against them or used as a source of malicious gossip. I can understand that. I never cease to be amazed at the number of destructive people there are who're only too delighted to pick up on others' weaknesses and make mileage out of them.

Yet sharing our worries and weaknesses with those we can trust is entirely liberating. It calls for a degree of honesty that, until we learn to trust, is both demanding and frightening. It's not, as some people think, a sign of feebleness but of strength, courage and realism. It also shows we're determined to turn our weakness into strength.

Airs and graces

There's a very beautiful prayer that asks God to forgive us for 'thinking of ourselves more highly than we ought to think'. It's a common enough failing but I'm not sure that many of us regard it as a sin.

The other day I was queuing patiently at a bus stop. (I must live on one of the most erratic routes in the country. The buses always seem to travel in convoy followed by an almighty gap.) However, my waiting time is never wasted. More often than not I can't help overhearing other people's conversations, and these can provide stimulation as well as great entertainment.

On this particular occasion, the two ladies in front of me had just spotted someone they knew on the other side of the road. They tried to attract her attention but failed. Then they decided they'd been snubbed.

'I don't know,' said one of them. 'Just who does she think she is? Walking by as though she owns the world! I knew her family when they had nothing.' There then followed some fairly harsh comments on the woman's background, bank account and current behaviour.

The moment that we put on airs and graces and start thinking of ourselves more highly than we ought, someone, somewhere, will pull us down to earth, and to be honest that's no bad thing. We should always be proud of our backgrounds even if we've come into money or found a new status in life. Humble origins are nothing to be ashamed of.

I now live in a world quite different from the one in which I was brought up. I can afford things my mother never could. In many ways I've a far easier life than she had. But I hope I'll never forget the sort of family I come from, nor the people who've helped me along the way.

Yes, we must have proper self-respect but that shouldn't license us to think of ourselves more highly than we ought.

Weighty matters

Perhaps I flatter myself in thinking I don't look it, but I'm actually overweight. Loose-fitting dog-collars and double-breasted suits may help to disguise the real me, but I've decided ten kilos must go.

First, I determined that I must exercise more. Although I walk a lot and rarely use the car in London, I don't run, jog or swim. I don't belong to an aerobics class. However, changes are in the pipeline. I've bought an exercise bike and a new pair of bathroom scales.

The shop assistant looked bemused when I asked for bathroom scales that wouldn't upset me. In the event I came away with scales that not only register my weight but also record my body fat.

The first time I stepped on them I had a big shock; fortunately, no one was in the house at the time. But it meant I could no longer ignore the truth. I was overweight.

The next problem was which diet to follow. Should I cut out bread? Should fruit and veg become the mainstay of my life? Should meat and alcohol be things of the past? Should I go for a crash diet or a slow burner?

All diets are difficult for me because I eat out so much. However, I do know that if I want to be fit, I have to do something about it. And this is as much a spiritual discipline as a physical one.

If you believe God became human in Jesus, then the body is as important as the soul and both must he cared for. We've been hearing recently about a new drug to help people lose weight. Although obesity is a serious medical problem for some, there are plenty of us who pile on the pounds simply because we fail to exercise self-control.

At certain times of year, such as Christmas, it's easy to overindulge. But if we do so, we must realize there's a price to be paid. Those of us who are able, and yet continually refuse, to take care of ourselves physically are guilty of misusing a precious part of God's creation – ourselves.

The biggest battle

Why can't they leave things alone? It seems nothing is sacred these days. Just as you get used to something, it's 'all change' and off we go again. And the Church is just as guilty. Nothing stays the same. Prayer books come and go, and as for hymn books, well, you only have to blink and a new one appears, with different tunes and changed words.

This certainly proved too much for journalist and church organist Richard Ingrams. With his fingers poised, he prepared to play the much-loved hymn *Onward Christian Soldiers*. The tune presented no problems – it was the old familiar one. But the words were far from familiar. No longer was the congregation to sing 'Onward Christian soldiers, marching as to war'. They had to put their heart, soul and voice into: 'Onward Christian pilgrims, up the rock way'.

To Richard, this was political correctness gone mad. To the compilers of the hymn book, it was a way of portraying a more positive and appropriate image. To me, it's a mixture of both. Some changes that are made in the interests of political correctness are silly, trivial and unnecessary. But I do think our images of faith have changed, and that needs to be reflected in the hymns we sing.

A warlike God figures prominently in the Old Testament. The battles that were fought in his name, the thousands slaughtered for the cause were meat and drink to its writers. But they're not part of the New Testament. And although some of the world's bloodiest battles have been fought in the name of religion, people are now thinking again about the value of war. Today, a world war would mean global destruction. So it's no wonder modern hymn writers emphasize peace rather than violence.

The only battle that still has to be fought is the battle against all that is evil. For that, Christians need to be joined by Jews, Buddhists, Sikhs and atheists. While evil still ravages the planet, none of us is safe. In this battle, no holds should be barred.

The whole story

Many people's knowledge of the Bible consists of edited highlights. Adam and Eve are generally well known, even if their significance isn't. Thanks to Tim Rice and Andrew Lloyd Webber, Joseph has become a firm favourite. Even if they don't recall that it was Moses to whom God gave the Commandments, most people know there are ten of them. Mind you, being asked to list all ten can cause a few problems.

Stories such as those about Noah's Ark, Jonah and the Whale, Samson and Delilah, and David and Goliath are also fairly familiar but, again, knowledge will still usually be confined to the edited highlights rather than the full story.

Take David and Goliath. Most people know about the little lad with a smooth stone in a sling who dealt a deadly blow to the mighty Philistine warrior. But how many know how the story develops from there?

When David returned in triumph to Saul, his master, he was received with open arms. However, it wasn't long before the mood changed and the reason for the change was jealousy. First, Saul was jealous of David's friendship with his son Jonathan. Second, as David went from strength to strength as commander of all the fighting forces, Saul became more and more jealous of his success. Even though Saul had appointed him commander, he still hated the adulation David received when he returned from yet another triumphant expedition. The fact that women used to chant, 'Saul struck down thousands but David tens of thousands,' was too much.

According to the story in 1 Samuel, Chapter 18, 'Saul was furious, and the words rankled. He said, "They have ascribed to David tens of thousands and to me only thousands. What more can they do but make him king?" From that time forward Saul kept a jealous eye on David.'

The following verse is even more telling: 'Next day an evil spirit from God seized Saul.' Saul was being tested and there is no greater test than jealousy. It really is an evil spirit because it is so destructive. It can destroy the jealous person and harm the victim of the jealousy.

In Saul's particular case, it was extremely damaging. Possessiveness and being unable to share in someone else's success, the twin elements of Saul's jealousy, are two of the most dangerous forms. Don't let them blight your life.

A safe haven

There are statistics and there are damned lies. But these statistics, I believe, are not only true, they're also frightening and tragic. They are about people who've been made to feel they don't belong. The office of the UN High Commissioner for Refugees says there are now more than 25 million people who have been forced to leave their countries. On top of that there are another 25 million who are internally displaced within their own countries and unable to return to their lands and villages. Ethnic cleansing, state-inspired terrorism and human rights abuse have taken their toll on over 50 million people.

The 30s and 40s were bad enough, with Hitler on the rampage, but the 90s were, if anything, worse. The people who could escape, did. This put pressure on other places. Certainly in Britain, Dover took the brunt of the influx of asylum seekers, which led to unpleasant scenes. Asylum seekers have become a political hot potato. But politicians and newspapers need to be very careful. They could find themselves stirring up feelings of hatred that easily get out of hand.

There will always be cheats and liars and they need to be weeded out, but the vast majority of refugees are people of integrity, courage and amazing discipline. They should not be treated like scum. They have been humiliated enough. They never wanted to be refugees. They would far prefer to be in their home country.

Caring for the true refugee is the responsibility of us all. If you are a Jew, you don't need any reminding of what it means to be a refugee. Christians also should be very sympathetic to the needs of refugees. After all, Jesus Christ himself, along with Mary and Joseph, became a refugee, seeking asylum in Egypt, at a very early age.

Outsiders have always been seen as a threat to society. It is when they're accepted that their true strengths are discovered.

The tourist trap

As the summer holiday season draws to a close, most of us will be looking back on glorious memories while others will be regretting their choice of destination or trying to recover from hours left in the lurch at airports. Hope will usually triumph over experience, however, and by next January many of us will again be poring over the brochures and planning our next trip.

We shouldn't forget that holidays were originally holy days and excursions were pilgrimages. Crowds flocked to shrines in the Holy Land, Assisi, Rome, Canterbury and even Winchester, where they paid respects to St Swithin, the patron saint of weather.

These were journeys with a purpose. Prayers needed to be offered, sins forgiven and blessings received. Often the travelling was both long and hard, and the only resting place was by the village well. Nowadays we complain if the airline meal isn't to our taste or if the flight is delayed.

Whereas pilgrims allowed time for their journey, we want to be there at once. After all, we're in a hurry with no time to waste. We rush from place to place taking photos but allow little time to appreciate our new surroundings.

To a certain extent the same is true of our modern attitude to faith. Setting aside time to understand and explore our beliefs is a thing of the past. We're into instant faith these days. If it doesn't work immediately we don't bother to try again. We also enjoy 'tasters', a little bit of this, a little bit of that. Any thought of real commitment frightens us off. We become faith tourists flitting from one attraction to another, never stopping to explore anything in depth. It's part of the 'six capitals in seven days' syndrome.

Children often find this difficult to understand. No longer taken to church or Sunday School and yet taught about religion in school, they very easily become confused. Parents may have their children baptized but that's as far as the commitment goes. And yet they're very annoyed if they're unable to get their child into a church school. What a muddled message this promotes!

The fact is that if you have this attitude to faith you're a tourist – and certainly not a pilgrim.

Spelling it out

What a brilliant invention! The little laptop computer on which I write these articles has a spell check, and the moment I make a mistake a red line comes under the particular word in question. All I have to do then is click onto my spell check and, as if by magic, the correct spelling appears on the screen. There's only one drawback. Every time I type the name 'Royle' a red line appears. It seems to think that there's only one 'Royal'.

Clever as this is, I do feel I'm cheating. I remember the days when, if I didn't know how to spell a word, I had to look it up in the dictionary and then write it out three times. As spelling was never my strongest point, I spent a great deal of time with my dictionary. However, it did teach me how to spell the word. Now, no effort is required, with the result that my spelling shows no sign of improvement.

All of us crave the easy life. Very few of us ever get it. But then a life without effort is often a life without meaning. It amazes me that some people think the moment they decide to believe in God, life will become effortless and all their problems will disappear. Some even think they'll get rich quick!

Where they get these ideas, goodness only knows. They certainly don't find them in either the Old or the New Testament. People such as Abraham, Moses, Elijah and Jeremiah had far from easy lives, and the disciples are warned by Jesus himself that if they want to follow him they'll have to 'take up their cross'.

It's through all the various tests, trials and tribulations of life that we grow as people. Provided we don't resent them and become bitter.

No one is promised an easy life. It's how we deal with its difficulties that really counts. Even so, I don't intend to stop using the spell check.

Question time

An inquisitive mind is one thing. A child who never stops asking questions is quite another.

How is it that children know, from a very early age, how to ask questions that either embarrass you or catch you off guard? And what gives them the energy to persist? Just when you think you have fobbed them off with a quick answer, back comes all the power of a supplementary query that has you completely floored. Imagine what Jeremy Paxman or John Humphrys were like as children! Their parents must have been driven nearly demented.

Questions about sex, God and creation are never far from any child's mind. They are fascinated by the world in which they are growing up and they always want to know more about it. And children's questions need to be taken seriously.

Jesus was constantly surrounded by people asking questions. Some of the questioners were out to trick him but that made no difference. Their questions were still taken seriously, even though many of them soon realized that, in questioning Jesus, they had bitten off more than they could chew.

Some questions received very detailed answers. Take the parable of the Good Samaritan. This story came about because some clever Dick of a lawyer tried to trick Jesus. 'What must I do to inherit eternal life?' he asked. Jesus replied with a question, 'What is written in the law?' Being a lawyer, the questioner was able to rattle off the 'legal' requirements, which involved loving God and loving your neighbour as yourself. Jesus commended him on his correct answer and said, 'Do this and you shall live.'

But the lawyer was determined to keep questioning. 'And who is my neighbour?' he asked. In reply, Jesus told him the story of the Good Samaritan. At the end of this parable he made the lawyer answer his own question. The lawyer had to decide who was the real neighbour to the person who fell among thieves. Jesus obviously didn't believe in handing out answers on a plate, especially to people who should know better. If you would like to read the story for yourself, it can be found in St Luke's Gospel, Chapter 10, verses 25–37.

Questions always need to be taken seriously, whoever they come from. But when you ask a question don't always expect an immediate answer. There are some things we have to work out for ourselves.

A call for help

Recently, thanks to a programme on Radio 2, I discovered the roots of the term 'strapping lad'. It comes from the world of bell-ringing. The tenor bell is so heavy that the ringer often requires further assistance from a lad who hangs on to the strap while the ringer deals with the rope. Hence, 'strapping lad'.

Another saying that always puzzled me is 'the weakest go to the wall'. I feared this referred to a dictatorial regime that lined up its weakest citizens against the wall and shot them. But I'd got it completely wrong.

The phrase's origins can be found in the Synagogue. Services are often quite long and, with no pews or chairs to sit on, the old, the very young and the infirm can find worship rather tiring. So it was suggested that they went to the wall to lean against it and draw on its support. It was a sign of compassion and caring that met a real need in a practical way.

Now I'm sure there were – and still are – some Jewish worshippers who would rather not admit that they need the support of a wall. And that's an attitude you'll find in every walk of life.

But admitting you need help is actually a sign of strength. Even Christ had to turn to others for help sometimes for such an everyday commodity as water. Without the help of Simon of Cyrene who carried his cross, he wouldn't have made the journey to Calvary.

Yet some people are too stubborn, arrogant or independent to ask for help, let alone accept any that is given. This isn't bravery. It often causes anxiety for those who really want to help and means that, when assistance is eventually accepted, the need for it has actually become more acute. Never be ashamed to ask for help.

Making an effort

At school, it was a long time before I won any prizes. Sporting trophies were out of the question and I wasn't that bright academically. However, in Form IV things took a turn for the better. I was awarded a prize for effort.

The Effort Prize went to the person who was unlikely to win a prize for anything specific. He was never fluent in French, nor was he marvellous in Maths or eloquent in English, but at least he tried. I came into that category. I was very trying!

Effort is, I believe, well worth rewarding. It is the opposite of sloth, one of the seven deadly sins, and I think that someone who's prepared to make an effort is also likely to value opportunities and try to make the most of them.

Nowhere is a bit of effort more needed than with prayer. There are times when prayer just happens, when you're so worried or so happy that you spontaneously offer a prayer to God. These are often referred to as arrow prayers. But in the main, prayer's a matter of patience, of persistence and of effort.

So many people give up praying when they don't get an instant result or answer. But praying isn't about instant answers; it's about being in a relationship with God. And as we know, no worthwhile relationship will flourish unless those involved are prepared to put some effort into it. This is one reason why so many marriages don't last. One or both parties don't make an effort. Of course, effort alone can't guarantee success, but at least they can always say, 'We tried.'

When Jesus was asked about prayer, he gave his disciples a pattern: The Lord's Prayer. You may have gabbled it as a child, but to pray it properly you have to make an effort. It's one well worth making. It stops you taking God's love for granted and makes you aware of your needs and shortcomings.

Don't spoil it

Picture the scene. It's been a very good day out. Everything's gone really well. There have been no traffic hold-ups. The weather's been just right. You managed to get the shopping done quickly. The people you wanted to see were in. Then, just as you're almost home, the children start to play up. They squabble over a toy and they're no longer prepared to be restrained by their seat-belts. What's been a perfect day is minutes away from descending into chaos. In your effort to maintain the peace, you utter the immortal words, 'You've behaved beautifully up until now so don't go and spoil it.'

If I'd been given a pound for every time that had been said to me as a child, I'd be a rich man. But it isn't only children who need to be told 'Don't go and spoil it.' We adults are pretty dab hands at spoiling things too.

Some people make a habit of it. They loathe to see people enjoying themselves. They are determined to cast a spell of gloom and doom over even the happiest occasions. They're a pain in the neck but really they should be pitied.

For most of us, though, it's a matter of not being able to sustain our good behaviour. I often think that Adam and Eve fell into this category. I'm sure the early days in the Garden of Eden were sheer bliss. But it just became too much for them to sustain. So instead of enjoying the gifts they'd been given, they had to go and spoil it. Mind you, as soon as they'd spoilt it, they realized what they'd done.

When we're about to spoil something, it wouldn't be a bad idea if we considered the implications of our actions first. Then we might be less ready to be so destructive and more anxious to hold fast to what is good.

5

Shelter and Protection

Although I enjoy cooking, fortunately I do get invited out to a great number of meals. At some I have to sing for my supper, at many it is a gathering of friends or family, but not infrequently I get invited to some of Britain's smartest hotels. One cold December night I had been dining at the Savoy. After an enjoyable evening of delicious food, fine wine and good company, I made my way to Embankment to catch the Tube. There, huddled in every doorway, were people in sleeping bags, under blankets, covered with cardboard trying to get a night's sleep. The contrast couldn't have been greater.

For me homelessness is the ultimate in lack of protection. No wonder the charity for the homeless calls itself Shelter and the one that works especially at Christmas, Crisis. If you have no home, it is a major crisis. You are denied the fundamental rights of shelter and protection. It hasn't got to be a mansion but as long as you have somewhere to go, shut your door and call your own, you have shelter.

Long before the British Parliament passed its Child Protection Bill, Christ had taught that children had a birthright to be protected. He was particularly clear as to what should happen to those who infringe that right. To the disciples' question as to who is the greatest in the Kingdom of Heaven, he has this to say: 'Whoever receives one such child in my name receives me, but whoever causes one of these little ones who believe in me to sin, it would be better for him to have a great millstone fastened round his neck and to be drowned in the depth of the sea.' There is little room for compromise there. But what goes for children, goes for adults as well. We are all God's children. We are all in need of protection.

It is when you know that you are protected that you can be yourself. You are free. It is when you are vulnerable that you are open to attack on all sides. When Jesus was in the wilderness he was at his most vulnerable. There was no shelter, nowhere to hide. Food, power and success are offered to him on a plate. But because of the inner protection that he has, he is able to resist. We too need to build up that inner protection so that when we are attacked, we also have the strength to defend ourselves.

Real religion

How well-versed are you on your Old Testament prophets? Isaiah, Elijah and Jeremiah may come to mind, but what about the lesser-known ones such Amos and Hosea – and Micah?

Recently I took another look at Micah. What I found was amazing, the best definition I know of real religion: Micah tells us that the Lord requires us 'to act justly and to love mercy and to walk humbly with God'.

There's nothing trivial or transitory about true faith or real religion, nor is it just a hot-water bottle for the soul. Real religion makes us question the way we behave and the standards by which we live. So let's do a little dissecting.

'To act justly': justice is a basic human right that many people feel they experience little of. Micah came from peasant stock and knew what it was to be treated unfairly by oppressive and unjust landowners. And, sadly, oppression doesn't only happen in the past. Bullying creeps into today's business practices, and thuggish behaviour on our roads is commonplace. If everyone acted justly, life would be better for all.

'To love mercy': there's nothing worse than seeing someone take revenge on someone else, especially when it concerns a wife and husband or, worse, parents with children. Revenge is cruel and destructive – no wonder we're told by God we should love mercy. When we show mercy we show our real strength, we show we're prepared to listen, to understand and forgive.

'To walk humbly with God': arrogance is a nasty trait in anyone, making them unapproachable. The truly humble person is one with inner strength, well aware of her or his own worth, who doesn't need to lord it over others.

When religion is defined in these terms, it's no longer a one-day-a-week job but something that underpins our whole lives.

Getting religion

Two readers have complained that there isn't enough about God in my articles. I disagree. My pieces are all about God. They may not be full of quotations from the Bible. They may not constantly call on the name of God. But they are still about God, our relationship with him, with one another and his world.

If you take the time to look at the teaching of Jesus, he wasn't always quoting the Holy Scripture or even the name of his Father. The parables of the Prodigal Son, the Good Samaritan and the lost coin are all human-interest stories. And yet, at the same time, they are deeply religious. The parables of the sower, the mustard seed and the wheat with the weeds are all agricultural stories that were appropriate for people who lived by the soil. And yet it's only after he's told the story that Jesus links them to the name of God and draws from them their religious significance.

Even in the Sermon on the Mount, Jesus used everyday illustrations such as lilies and lustful looks to teach eternal truths. Obviously, there were times when he quoted from Scripture to support his point, but his main concern was to teach in such a way that even those whose knowledge of Holy Writ was limited wouldn't feel excluded.

For me, life is spiritual. I believe that, as well as being a child of God, I'm also living in God's world and there's nothing in my life that's not God's, whether I mention his name or not.

Nor do I believe that God only works through Christians. There have been times when I've felt the presence of God through people who either belong to another faith or have none. If that's true for me, then it was true for Jesus.

It's easy to use the name of God and think that we're being religious, but it's as well to remember that, 'Not everyone who says unto me, Lord, Lord, shall enter the Kingdom of Heaven, but he who does the will of my Father who is in Heaven.' Actions mean more than words.

Is nothing sacred?

As most of my underpants are dedicated to St Michael, the news that Marks & Sparks was in difficulties came as quite a shock. And as I queued with my heavily laden trolley at Sainsbury's, I couldn't understand why their profits were down too.

Then, when I heard that the Walt Disney organization was having a rethink because of fierce competition, I thought, 'Is nothing sacred?' It didn't take me long to come up with the answer. No 'thing' is sacred.

Only God and people, who are made in God's image, are sacred. That is why there's little point in putting your trust in your possessions. Material things have a limited lifespan. They may add happiness, style and a bit of sparkle to our lives but in the end, they are just things, and no thing is sacred. So why judge people by the things they have? It's a waste of time. It's the sort of people they are that really counts.

The moment you look on people as sacred, your attitude towards them changes. This isn't to say we're all perfect. We certainly aren't. But we are sacred and need to be treated as such. The moment you start looking on others as sacred is the moment that you stop using or abusing them and start to respect them. The moment you start to see yourself as sacred is the moment you stop rejecting or abusing yourself. So many difficulties stem from not having the right love or respect for *yourself*. It's no wonder we don't respect others.

However, it's only when we have a right respect for God, who is eternally sacred, that we can ever hope to get the rest of our lives into perspective. We will get angry with God. There will be times when we feel he's light years away. Yet it's only when we acknowledge we are his children and are loved by him that we will be able to build our lives on foundations that are solid and sacred.

Pointers to God

A Gideon Bible in a hotel room comes as no surprise to me. And I shouldn't have been surprised when, in a hotel room in Cairo, I opened my dressing table drawer and found, instead of a Bible, an arrow pointing in the direction of Mecca. After all, I was in a Muslim country and many Muslims take seriously the five times set aside for daily prayer offered in the direction of the Holy City of Mecca. This arrow got me thinking. For a Muslim it was more than pointing in a certain geographical direction, it was a pointer to God. However, we don't need to be a Muslim or in a Cairo hotel to look for a pointer to God; it should be part of everyday life.

The first pointer to God must be the love we have as wives, husbands, fathers, mothers, brothers, sisters or children. The love within the family must be a reflection of God's love for each one of us.

That is why it is so sad when families fall apart. It is a shattering of that reflection. And although God's love is always there, it remains shattered until such wounds are bound up and scars are healed.

The second pointer to God must be the acts of thoughtfulness and kindness that are shown to us, sometimes by the most unexpected people in the most unexpected places. These reflect the acts of kindness that Jesus received, not just from those who were close to him, like Martha and Mary, but the kindness of people regarded as outcasts, like Samaritans, sinners and tax gatherers.

The third pointer to God must be the world in which we live, which we believe is God's own creation. Here again, there is defacement and defilement, but the world itself is beautiful. It is our duty to make sure that this beauty is revealed and not hidden by the destructiveness of we human beings.

I've given you three pointers to God – there are obviously many more. But above all each one of us is called to be a pointer to God in the way that we live our lives, show our love and exercise our gifts.

Differing routes

The other day I was on the London Underground on my way to see a couple about their wedding. Opposite me were two men who'd obviously come from different parts of the country to meet up.

'We must arrange another meeting,' said the elder of the two, getting out his diary. 'Certainly,' said the other, reaching for his electronic organizer.

To me that was a parable in the making. I was thrilled that it was the man with the old-fashioned diary who sorted himself out first. But then that's only personal prejudice on my part. In the end, the man with the very latest in electronic gadgets had caught up and a date was fixed. Both men had the same aim, it was just that they had different ways of going about it.

In our approach to God many of us take different routes. Although, as you know, I believe the different Christian denominations are a luxury we can't afford, in the end we all worship the same Christ. It's very important that we're able to express our love and worship of God in ways that make sense to us. The Quakers are drawn to God through silence, the Methodists through hymn-singing, the Roman Catholics through ritual.

I know that's a very simplistic way of putting things, but it holds more than an element of truth. At times, I'm drawn to worship God in the quietness of a thinly attended early morning Communion Service. At other times, a full-blown Choral Cathedral Eucharist feeds my soul with spiritual strength. We're all different and we all have different needs, both physically and spiritually.

This truth also needs to be carried through to people of other faiths. The fact that I recognize other faiths in no way diminishes my belief in the uniqueness of Jesus Christ. But just as Jesus was a Jew and drew on the strength of foreigners, so I believe that all of us can draw on the strengths of faiths other than our own.

When I read the Psalms I feel linked with all those Jews who, in synagogues around the world, are using exactly the same words and thoughts for their worship. As I spend time in meditation I give thanks for the way in which the Buddhists have made all of us look again at this powerful way of prayer. These are just two examples. There are many more.

The worship of Almighty God should be the aim of all of us. In no way must we belittle those who use a different route to achieve that objective.

Who's in charge?

Some car stickers are amusing, while others are just plain confusing. For instance, the other day I noticed one that should really have given me supreme confidence but in fact had quite the opposite effect. It read, 'Relax, God is in charge'.

That's all very well, I thought, but it isn't God sitting behind the wheel, and even if it was, I'm not at all sure what sort of driver he would be.

It's absolutely true, God is in charge of his creation, but that doesn't mean we should sit back and let everything happen. If our farmers adopted that policy very few churches would be celebrating Harvest Festival this autumn. Gardeners who leave everything to God, rather than carefully cultivating flowers and shrubs, tend to reap a chaotic wilderness.

We're not puppets completely under God's control. We've been given talents and free will and it's up to us to use them properly. Our relationship with God is that of a partnership, and he expects us to keep to our part of the bargain.

Yes, there are times when God will provide. But it's no good using that as an excuse to do nothing ourselves. It's true that God heals, but healing is more often brought about by the skill of doctors and nurses than by celestial intervention. God can show us the way, but often he prefers us to work things out for ourselves so that we can be accountable for our actions.

The message 'Relax, God is in charge' persuades me to keep my distance in this case. This driver seems to have handed responsibility over to God, avoiding the need to concentrate on the finer points of the Highway Code.

The truth is that we can only relax and accept the fact that God is in charge when we are taking full responsibility for our own lives. Otherwise I think we may find God saying to us, 'You're on your own, mate!'

Our real home

The British have always been great explorers. Deepest Africa and furthest India turned pink on the atlas. Australia, New Zealand and America fascinated the British explorer despite the dangers involved. Shipwrecks, starvation and sickness all took their toll.

Now, things have changed. Armed with a passport, injections, visas and an airline ticket, the world's our oyster. Unless we're balloonists, we no longer explore – we travel. Despite the fact that we want to see different places, we want most things to remain the same. There are great moans if the traditional British breakfast isn't on offer. After all, we only have a cooked breakfast on holiday. And as for any other nationality's tea-making abilities, forget it! No one makes a better cup of tea than the British.

In my experience, the Americans are just as bad. That's why so many of their hotel chains are practically identical. Wherever they are in the world, they want to feel at home. It's the Antipodean travellers who are more adventurous, especially the young ones. They take what they find.

The real difference comes when people open their mouths and speak. English is widely spoken around the globe, but we shouldn't expect it to be. We can get by with the aid of a phrase book, but we're in trouble if there's a different script. Have you ever tried reading a street sign in Russian?

That's when you realize you're in a different land, surrounded by a different people. Their early years in Egypt made the Israelites aware of what it was like to be strangers in a foreign land. Then, during the Exile, they were constantly reminded of the difficulties faced by foreigners. 'By the waters of Babylon we sat down and wept', begins Psalm 137.

In the New Testament we're told that on this earth we have no abiding city. We don't belong here. We're strangers. Our real home is with God. So be careful about making yourself too comfortable in this world, when it's really the next world we should be preparing for.

Family ties

Woman's Weekly has a reputation for looking after the soul as well as the body. Liz Burn's tried-and-tested recipes make sure the body is well fed and, hopefully, my column, set among your letters, keeps an eye on the well-being of your soul. Certainly a reader in Burnley thinks so.

In a letter to the Editor, Miss M. Heap generously expressed her gratitude. Now, it's always nice to read a letter of thanks, but in this case the writer's name was even more important. You see, my mother's maiden name was Heap too. Rather thoughtlessly, her parents called her Agnes, so when she signed herself A. Heap, her helpful schoolmates would add 'of rubbish'.

On receiving a copy of Miss Heap's letter, I immediately phoned my Auntie Do in Lancashire, who was also a Miss Heap. She said she didn't know of a Miss M. Heap in Burnley, but thought that there were two Heaps in Prestwich.

Family names never ever lose their power to attract because despite what anyone may say, the family is still the most important unit in our lives.

To Jewish people, the family is of paramount importance, and St Matthew, writing for a Jewish readership, began his Gospel with a family tree to show that not only was Jesus descended from David, but his roots went back as far as Abraham. You don't get more Jewish than that.

When family ties break, there are only losers. The pain reaches deep into the soul. There may be relief at times – no one can stand constant physical or mental abuse, and unfaithfulness puts great pressure on a family – but when the break occurs there's a sense of failure.

The family is under more pressure than ever. People live miles apart, jobs are insecure, expectations are high. So family ties must become bonds of love, providing the protection and security we all need.

Bless this house

I know I'm beginning to sound like Victor Meldrew from *One Foot in the Grave*, but you'll never believe it! After a busy morning, I was returning home to prepare two talks I was due to give the next day. As I turned the corner of my road, I noticed a 'For Sale' sign on what should have been my neighbour's house. Drawing nearer, I realized it was my house up for sale! I was livid and went and told the estate agents exactly what I thought of them straight away.

It was only after I'd made a cup of tea and cooled down a bit that I realized why I was so angry. It was the thought, albeit irrational, that my house could be sold over my head without my even being consulted. I hate it when I hear of someone's home being repossessed. It doesn't matter whether you live in a palace or a bedsit, your home is your security and to have it taken away is a devastating experience.

However, it's our own responsibility to create the atmosphere within our homes. At the end of a wedding service, I generally add a prayer for the home that the newly married couple set up together. I pray it will be a home of love, sympathy and understanding, where people are accepted for who they are and not what they might be. I also pray it may be a disciplined home, where people are treated with respect. For me, a good home welcomes friends and strangers. After my mother died, I found I was very dependent on the friendship of others. Fortunately, I was never short of people prepared to open their homes to me, something I hope I never took for granted and for which I'll always be grateful.

At the end of my wedding prayer, I pray that the home may be one where Christ is always present and welcome. A true home is a deeply spiritual place, where we know we're loved and are given the strength to love others. But for this to happen we really do need to ask God to 'bless this house'.

Water of life

It'll be a while before I know whether I've done the right thing or not, but I've just had my house fitted with a water meter. Well, they were being offered free and, with my eye for a bargain, I thought I'd be silly not to accept.

However, I'm not totally convinced that I'll actually save money. Living alone I should, but there's no guarantee. I often have people to stay, which means more sheets and towels to wash. Although I never use the dishwasher when I'm at home alone, I do entertain quite often and that's when the dishwasher really comes into its own.

Having the meter has certainly made me far more water conscious. It's so easy to take it for granted. When we turn on the tap, we rarely think about the millions of people for whom it's a struggle to find and store water. We should never forget that water is a wonderful resource, a part of God's creation without which we could not survive, physically or spiritually.

Water has always had tremendous spiritual power: from the parting of the Red Sea, to the storm that was stilled on the Sea of Galilee; from the waters of the Flood, to those of the River Jordan in which Jesus was baptized; from the water that Jesus changed into wine at the wedding in Cana, to the water Pilate used to wash his hands of all responsibility.

Uncontrolled, it can destroy, but with its power harnessed, it can sustain and refresh. Water also has enormous symbolic significance, as Jesus made clear when he used it to wash the disciples' feet and when he promised to give the woman at the well 'living water' with which she would never thirst.

So when we wash in the morning or prepare ourselves for bed at night, I suggest that as we splash water on our faces, we take time to consider those matters in our lives that need destroying and those that need refreshing. We will then leave the bathroom not just physically but spiritually cleansed as well.

In the mood

I saw it. I liked it. I bought it. I was in America recording some radio programmes for the BBC when my eye was caught by a T-shirt in a shop window with this message: 'Next mood swing in only 6 minutes. Please stand by'. I had to buy it because I knew the moment I put it on I'd feel good. Bad moods would disappear and I'd be in the frame of mind to tackle all that the day could throw at me.

Children are very good at being 'in a mood'. You can tell their mood from their faces. Bright eyes and a smile show all's going well. A dropped jaw with a pouting mouth means beware: doors could well be slammed and as for a civil word, you might as well forget it!

Coaxing children out of their bad moods is normally fairly easy. A little negotiating, a bit of bribery and the job's done. Not so with adults. Once we're 'in a mood' it takes more than a tube of Smarties to move us.

There are days when it feels as though we've got out of the wrong side of the bed. The weather's grim. Thoughts of what the day holds fill us with fear. Other people seem to be very unco-operative. Everything goes wrong or takes longer than expected. A drink to drown our sorrows only revives them and, generally, the best thing is to get back into bed and call it a day. But that's not often possible.

St Paul, I believe, must have been quite a moody person. He wasn't easy to travel with, and in his discussions with Peter he didn't like to be wrong. But he knew that if he was to have any impact on the people he met he'd have to put his own feelings behind him and concentrate on their needs rather than his.

He also realized his bad moods would be overcome if he incorporated the mind of Jesus into his own. And that's easier said than done. It can only come about if prayer becomes an integral part of our lives rather than an optional extra. Moodiness is overcome by putting ourselves regularly in the presence of God and putting the needs of others before our own.

In proportion

In the current sensitive climate I am not at all sure that some over-zealous people wouldn't have accused Jesus of child abuse. After all, he did once get hold of a child and stand him by his side so that he could teach his disciples about humility. There is no record that he knew the child or that the child was related to him. All it says in St Luke's Gospel is that an argument arose among the disciples as to which of them was the greatest, and when Jesus perceived the thoughts of their hearts, 'he took a child and put him by his side'. You can imagine the fuss that would cause today.

Every child has the right to be protected, and Jesus had uncompromising words for those people who either hurt children or lead them astray. But the pendulum seems to have swung too far the other way. People are now scared stiff even of talking to children in case they are thought to be a paedophile. Even parents are not safe. Not so long ago, a television newsreader and her husband had an accusing finger pointed at them because they took photographs of their children in the bath. I don't think that there can be a family photo album in the land that hasn't got a picture of a naked child either in the bath or by a paddling pool or even on a rug. These are totally innocent pictures taken to remember a particular stage of a child's life.

School teachers daren't put an arm round a child's shoulder to comfort them when they are crying, for fear of their action being misinterpreted. Care workers who often have to wash and toilet children who are disabled have an even more difficult task. People in parks who used to love watching children need to sit far away from playgrounds in case their motives are questioned.

Let's get things back in proportion. Children must be protected – but those who love children in an open and honest way should not be made to feel they are criminals.

Direct line

All of a sudden the word 'direct' seems to be everywhere. You can get direct banking and insurance. Catalogues offer clothes direct and, according to the ads, you can save money by booking your holidays direct.

However, there's nothing new about getting God direct. That has been possible ever since we discovered the power of prayer. We may not get a friendly voice at the end of the phone saying, 'Good morning. Tracy speaking. How may I help you?' but we will get the chance to celebrate our happiness, apologize for our stupidity and share our concerns for those we love.

The difference between prayer and the modern idea of direct is that today's version is meant to make life easier, simpler, less demanding and cheaper. Prayer is none of those. It's hard, often complicated, always demanding and never cheap. Too many people use prayer as a last resort rather than as the power underpinning their lives.

First and foremost, prayer is about forging a relationship. Tracy may strike up a temporary connection with you on the phone, but as soon as your call is over, she's on to the next customer. But our relationship with God is permanent. We're always in his presence and always protected by his love. We are, after all, his children.

Although there are occasions when we have to shoot what I call 'arrow' prayers to God, for a sustained and purposeful 'prayerlife' it's essential to set aside time. No relationship, human or divine, is going to survive casual acquaintance. Prayer also needs to reflect all of our life and not just our needs. Nothing is more irritating than the child who constantly says, 'I want, I must have.' Or even one who insists, 'Please help, please, please help!'

Only a relationship that reflects every aspect of life will get you in touch with God direct and, what's more important, it will make sure you stay in touch.

6

Storm and Tempest

Over 35 years ago I set sail on a five-week-and-two-day voyage to Australia. My fellow travellers were all people looking for a new start in life. According to the adverts they were about to 'Walk tall down under'. On the first Sunday at sea a few of the faithful gathered for the morning service. The following week, a few more. By week three reality was beginning to set in. There was concern as to whether they had made the right choice. Also the weather had changed and the sea had become much rougher. Suddenly there was a marked increase at the numbers attending the Sunday morning service.

There was a new urgency to the way the congregation sang the hymn *Eternal Father, Strong to Save*, especially the two lines:

From rock and tempest, fire and foe,
Protect them wheresoe'er they go.

Storms feature prominently in the Bible. Jonah gets caught in one. St Paul seems to be a particularly unfortunate traveller. And Jesus himself is caught in a storm but he sleeps right through it. Jonah is rescued by the whale. St Paul's final voyage to Rome was especially hazardous. Against his advice they had set sail and had sailed straight into a storm. Trying to lighten the load they ditched the ship's cargo and tackle. For 14 days they were drifting helplessly in the Adriatic. Taking soundings they found that the water was getting shallower and shallower and that they were heading straight for the rocks. Fearing they would be shipwrecked they did the only sensible thing to do. They let out four anchors from the stern, and prayed for day to come.

Some of the 276 crew wanted to abandon ship. Paul advised them not to. This time they listened to him. Instead they fed themselves, regained their strength and daylight did come. But even then it wasn't plain sailing. Fortunately the centurion, who was responsible for the ship, its crew and the prisoners, took charge, gave clear orders and not a single life was lost.

I am reminded of that story every time I am on an aircraft, we hit turbulence and the seat belt signs are switched on. There is nothing you can do. Those who can do something are doing it and you just have to put your faith in them, sit tight and ride out the storm. It is frightening but, more often than not, daylight does come. Damage may be done but storms do pass.

Destructive attitude

When the highly controversial film *Hilary and Jackie* was doing the rounds, it looked as though the musical genius of the superb cellist Jacqueline du Pré was about to be lost in the claims and counter-claims about her personal life. To me it was very self-indulgent of her sister and brother to write the book they did. By all means talk to a therapist, a wise person or a trusted friend, but to take that sort of dirty linen to the most public wash place on earth – the media – was not on.

It was more than interesting that Jacqueline's husband, Daniel Barenboim, refused to join the dirty-linen washers. Doubtless it was out of respect for his highly talented wife, who later became a broken woman under the destructive power of multiple sclerosis. However, it wasn't only the MS that was destructive. So was the attitude of Jacqueline's brother and sister, Piers and Hilary. According to John Williams, the celebrated guitarist and personal friend of Jacqueline, Piers and Hilary had told their sister her MS was 'God's punishment for leaving Christ'. Jacqueline had converted to Judaism when she married Barenboim.

The thought that God would use such a way of punishing one of his children is total anathema to me. How can a loving God use such a crippling disease to control his people? The Old Testament is full of people being punished, for that was how the people at that time viewed any misfortune. However, Jesus tried to correct that way of thinking in the New Testament.

There are times when a wrong way of life can bring on illness, but that's not God's punishment. That's the result of our way of life. I would give up on God if I thought that the young disabled people I've met over the years were given their disability as a way of punishing either them or their parents. To me that's totally inconceivable, as the very idea creates a monster, not a God. I don't hesitate in saying that coupling sickness and suffering with God's punishment is wrong. Full stop.

Power drivers

Have you noticed the number of women who drive 4×4 vehicles, even though they may not see a dirt track from one year's end to another? You may be one of them.

These cars are obviously very useful for the school run but this is a time when, unfortunately, drivers are often at their worst. They totally disregard any parking – or even stopping – instructions, despite the fact that they're putting their children's lives at risk and probably bringing other drivers to the verge of road rage.

But I'm digressing! Apparently women like this type of vehicle because it gives them a sense of power. From their position high up in the driver's seat they can keep their heads above other cars and ward off any silly, selfish men who think it's fun to harass a female driver.

Power is a much sought-after commodity, and in today's competitive society few survive without it. But don't you think we've gone a little power-mad? For all I know, you may well be into power-dressing but in the end, unless you have personal authority, it won't matter what you drive or what you wear. Because power without authority is, ultimately, useless.

That was the problem faced by the religious leaders at the time of Jesus. They knew every rule in the book and, believe me, the Old Testament book Leviticus is not short of the odd rule or two. And what's more, they weren't reluctant to enforce them. For instance, carrying beds on the Sabbath – forbidden; healing the sick on the Sabbath – forbidden; plucking an ear of corn on the Sabbath – forbidden. Whatever the action, if it was forbidden, the offender was punished. So yes, they weren't short of power but they had very little authority. It must have been really galling for them to see the people flock to Jesus, a man with no power but packed with natural authority.

Parents, teachers, police, politicians, even clergy – all no longer automatically have the power that they once had. Their position doesn't give them power. They only get real power when they're seen as people with personal authority. And that's just as it should be.

Shifting the blame

I thought I knew the Adam and Eve story off by heart. The other day, I discovered I didn't. I was rereading it in preparation for a recording I was making for Lincoln Cathedral and, as I did so, all the characters in the story struck me as the biggest load of blame shifters I'd ever come across.

When Adam is caught with not just his trousers down in the Garden of Eden, he doesn't only blame Eve for the predicament he's in – he also blames God: 'The woman whom you gave to be with me, she gave me the fruit of the tree and I ate.'

In other words, 'If you, God, hadn't landed me with this woman in the first place, I wouldn't be in the mess I'm in now.' At least Eve doesn't blame God for creating the serpent, but she certainly wasn't prepared to take responsibility for her own actions either.

Just as blame shifting is a feature of the very first chapters in the Bible, so it plays a predominant part in our early lives. I'm sure all of us with brothers or sisters have tried to land them in the mire with our parents rather than face the music ourselves. Certainly, at school shifting the blame should be an ingredient in the National Curriculum. It's part of the essential survival kit of any pupil. But sooner or later it has to stop. We can't go on shifting the blame for the whole of our lives. The music has to be faced and responsibility for our actions must be taken.

Of course, it's much easier to blame our parents, our teachers, our upbringing or our environment for any weaknesses in our character. But if we want to be treated as mature adults we must have the strength and courage to take responsibility for the people we are and the things we do.

For some people life is obviously easier than it is for others, but that shouldn't stop us from being in control of our own lives and answerable to both God and other people for all we do.

Our changing earth

The 'silly season' of the press was dominated by two stories that were anything but silly. One was the stressful situation as regards asylum seekers and the other was an earthquake in Turkey.

Despite the odd glimmer of hope when, beyond expectation, another person was rescued from the rubble, the story was one of tears, sweat, destruction, anxiety, criticism and hopelessness. Cowboy builders and disorganized officials were blamed. The only person who seemed to get off scot-free was God. Many devout Muslims saw the devastation as the will of Allah and accepted it. But for many, the question must be, 'How does a loving God allow such terrible things to happen?'

I don't believe that it's God's will that thousands should die, be left homeless or suffer. But he does expect us to treat his creation with respect. We now know, better than ever before, where the seismic areas of the world are. Through our scientific knowledge we can keep a constant eye on them. But we don't. Jerry-built buildings are thrown together in places where it's known that danger lurks, because people are greedy for profit. People should live in the strongest buildings in such areas, but because the people are often poor, they're exploited. You can't blame God for that.

Isn't it time we took creation seriously? Creation was not a once-and-for-all thing that just happened in six days – it's a continuing process. Sometimes these changes are brought about by us. At last we're beginning to realize the part we've played in global warming. But volcanoes erupt, the cliffs crumble, the sea erodes, the sun evaporates and the earth moves and shakes. All this is continuing creation.

There's something wonderful about God's creation but it's a wonder also tinged with awe. We neglect its rules at our peril. All of us will suffer if we continue to abuse it. That certainly isn't the will of God.

Destination unknown

There's no better way of getting around London quickly than on the Underground, even if, by the end of the day, you feel like a mole.

Although I live on what's called 'The Misery Line', there are signs of improvement. Most stations now have electronic indicators telling you the destination and arrival time of the next train. However, there is a snag – every so often it appears that no one has a clue as to where the next train's going. The indicator flashes, 'Check destination on the front of the train.'

Still, in all fairness, it's not only London Underground that needs to check its destinations. Many of us, from time to time, aren't quite sure where we're going, why we're going or when we'll get there.

Under God's guidance, men and women have always sought to travel towards a Promised Land. But such a journey, as Moses and the Children of Israel found to their cost, is never very easy. There are often obstacles to be overcome. They may not be as daunting as the Red Sea, but then the solution may not be as easy, either. And having overcome the obstacles, there's the possibility that, like Moses, you may not make it. But that shouldn't stop you trying.

The person who travels through life with little or no idea of where they're going or what they want to achieve often ends up wondering what they've done with all their years.

At one time, everything seemed so much easier – our lives were mapped out from the word go. But now we have far greater choice – we've endless opportunities to plan things for ourselves. But with choice comes responsibility.

In setting our sights on a particular goal we can be selfish and search only for personal fulfilment. This is very short-sighted. Our destinations need to be set with others in mind, so when they're reached it means we've also brought fulfilment and happiness to others.

No place for hatred

After my initial anger had worn off, I felt very sorry about the 'Whites Only' organ transplant donor. As I did when, only the next day, I read about the 'Asians Only' organ transplant donor. In the 'Asians Only' case the organs were refused, and rightly so, even though it meant up to six people were denied life-saving operations. But leaving aside whether such racist conditions should be listened to, let alone accepted, I felt so sorry that anyone living or dead could have such anger, hatred, bitterness or meanness in their heart that they could actually ask that their organs, or the organs of a loved one, should be given to a white person only.

It's doubly sad because obviously these people are not without care. They were willing to use their suffering to relieve the suffering of others. They wanted the death of the person they loved to bring life, or at least a fuller life, to someone else. This is both good and generous. When you think of the number of people waiting for transplants, all of us need to be a little more thoughtful. To bring life and hope to others is a wonderful thing to do. We should all carry a donor card.

The tragedy is that their generosity was so restricted. I don't know the background of either of these cases. It could well be that they'd had difficult relations with someone of another race, colour or creed. But nothing justifies carrying such bitterness beyond the grave. Death really does continue to have a sting and the grave will always be the victor if we use it as a weapon against our fellow men and women.

No one has the right to say to whom an organ should be given (unless, of course, they're giving it to a named relative or friend). No hospital or doctor has the right to accept such preconditions. There shouldn't need to be a law about this. It should be a part of our living and dying together as fellow human beings. But unfortunately, you can't rely on natural goodness. The evil of which each one of us is capable can all too easily get the upper hand. When this is the case, then the law must step in or people's personal wishes should be ignored or refused.

When the truth hurts

My heart sinks the moment someone says, 'You won't want to hear this, but ...'. You can be sure that something unpalatable is on its way. It may be something relatively unimportant – they can't get you tickets for a particular event you want to see, or the flight to the sun you had hoped to take is fully booked. On the other hand, it could be something far more serious, especially when it is part of a heart-to-heart discussion.

Telling people what they didn't want to hear was the job of the prophets in the Old Testament. They saw it as their job to let people know the whole picture, which included spelling out very clearly both the consequences of their actions and the weaknesses in their characters. No punches were pulled and sensitivity took second place to directness. The prophets felt that the Children of Israel needed to get the message and to get it straight. They felt totally secure in what they were saying, as they had the authority of God behind them.

For us, it isn't so easy and yet, at times, it is something we have to do. Frightened of treading on toes or hurting feelings, things that need to be said are often left unsaid. So situations remain unchanged and resentment builds up. Obviously, it rarely helps if things are said insensitively – but nor does it help if they're not said at all.

Just as it isn't easy to say things that other people don't want to hear, so it is very difficult to hear things that you don't want to hear. And yet, if we are to grow as people we must. The truth may hurt, but it can be the foundation of a new beginning and a better person.

It rarely helps a person to be told something they don't want to hear in the middle of a flaming row, but if they are told it in love, then it may not be easy to say but it is much easier to hear.

Hidden temptations

For some, the sight of an unlocked car or an unzipped handbag is an invitation to steal. Even if they didn't set out with the intention, the temptation proves too hard to resist. Just the glimmer of an opportunity leads them into sin and crime.

For most of us, however, temptation is far more subtle. The most famous temptations of all, those of Jesus in the wilderness, are certainly reported in a most obvious and dramatic way – turning stones into bread, giving in to false gods or jumping off a parapet of the Temple are all sensational stunts and easily recognizable. But it's the meanings behind them that are most significant, the testing of Jesus' commitment and loyalty. The obvious can usually be recognized and avoided but hidden temptations are really destructive.

Greed comes in many shapes and sizes, that extra cream cake being the least significant. The constant desire for more possessions, even when we don't want or need them, is a temptation that knows no bounds. Trying to be bigger and better can, in the end, make us look very small. Frightened we might be powerless and at the mercy of others, we'll stop at nothing to make sure we're not the underdog.

We all have to learn that human power is transitory and will pass away. The only power worth recognizing is the power of God, but the temptation to put him to the test is very real. As children, we push our parents to the limits, seeing just how far we can go. As adults, we try the same game with God, pushing him to prove that he loves us. It may be more subtle than the way we tested our parents but, ultimately, it has the same effect, an undermining of basic trust and belief.

With a little moral strength and courage, temptations that stare you in the face can be resisted. It's the hidden ones that you really need to guard against.

The right direction

Arriving by air in any foreign country is never easy, especially if you're travelling alone. Just finding the way out can be an ordeal, let alone coping with immigration and customs. However, when I arrived in Jordan things couldn't have been easier. As I stepped off the plane there was a man waiting for me. He took me through all the formalities and introduced me to the person who would be looking after me. 'Here's your guide for the next five days,' he said. 'His name's Jesus.'

There was no answer to that! Throughout my life I've tried to use Jesus as my guide. But it hasn't been easy. The demands are great and they're not always as straightforward as we'd like. The young lawyer who wants to know how he can inherit eternal life is told the parable of the Good Samaritan. The person who wants to know whether he should pay tax or not is told to go and get a coin and see whose inscription is on it. The people who are determined to find out by what authority Jesus teaches are set a real conundrum about John the Baptist.

So one of the first things I learnt about Jesus' leadership is that he doesn't hand you everything on a plate. He expects you to think for yourself. As a guide, he adopts the practice of the Palestinian shepherd – he goes in front of his flock, so he's the first to meet danger. He certainly doesn't shield you from danger, but he does share it with you. He also shows you how suffering can be transformed, that goodness can come out of even the worst situation.

For me, this is the core of the crucifixion. It isn't allowed to be the end. It's taken and transformed by the resurrection. It shows that from sorrow can come joy; from death can come life. When we have these thoughts as our guide, then we must be heading in the right direction.

Lessons in leadership

Only once have I acted as a holiday courier but, I can assure you, never again. Admittedly I only had 22 people to look after. But they were all different. They had different needs, different expectations, and it was my job to make sure that they were all happy and safe. There was one elderly couple who were a dream to look after. For them, this was the holiday of a lifetime and they were determined to enjoy everything they saw. And they did. They were even thrilled when they saw a box of Typhoo teabags in an Arab market.

But not everyone was so easily pleased. One couple loathed foreign food. For another couple, their room was never right. One gentleman had trouble with the plumbing in every hotel we stayed in, and one pair made a speciality out of constantly being the last people to get back on the coach. No matter what time you asked them to be there, they were always ten minutes late.

If I had problems with 22 people, it's no wonder Moses had an almost impossible task with the Children of Israel. They grumbled about almost everything. They even thought of abandoning their own God. They must have been, like most big groups, a real nightmare, yet Moses remained faithful to the calling he'd been given by God. If ever there was an example of 'when the going gets tough, the tough get going', it was Moses.

But then, being a leader is never easy. It doesn't matter whether you're running a home, an office, a factory, a school or a hospital, the moment you're required to show leadership qualities, that's the moment people will start to question you and your abilities. There'll be times when you'll be able to say 'because I say so', but sooner or later even that won't work, especially with your children. There's only one way to show real leadership and that's by example. Once family, friends and colleagues know they can trust you they'll follow you. But they won't necessarily make it easy for you.

Follow my leader

My music teacher at school was the first person to think that I had leadership potential. Long before the days of transistors, when electrical equipment was very heavy, I was sent, with another boy, to collect the school gramophone. Fortunately the other boy was much stronger, so I suggested he carried the equipment and I would open the doors. I arrived back in class as fresh as a daisy; he was exhausted. It was then the music master decided I was a born leader: in other words, I'd organize other people but wasn't keen to get my hands dirty!

Over the years the role of leader has become much more demanding. No longer do people do just as they're told. Everything is questioned and yet the leader is still held responsible should anything go wrong.

I wasn't at all surprised to hear that the Guide Association was finding it hard to recruit new leaders. Who wants to be responsible for other people these days? I've nothing but respect for those men and women who give up their evenings and weekends to encourage and guide young people.

However, without adult leaders it's the young who suffer. It's a great pity more people don't volunteer to help those organizations that do so much to shape our children's futures. If you're able to help yet aren't willing to do so, please don't complain about the behaviour of today's youngsters.

Jesus saw himself very much as a leader, as 'the Good Shepherd' who led his flock. He didn't try to round them up, he went ahead, seeing the dangers and difficulties before they came. He protected them from wolves and, more importantly, from false shepherds.

We're all called to be a leader – as parent, partner, teacher, friend or workmate. Real leadership is given by example. It's not something to be left only to the bosses.

The best-laid plans

It was going to be a busy day, so it had to be well planned. I'd decided to get up at 5 a.m. and do an early morning shop at the supermarket as I couldn't afford to waste time hanging about at the tills. For once I'd even written a shopping list. Then it was in the car for a 120-mile journey to a birthday lunch with a 90-year-old, stopping on the way to buy flowers. But that wasn't all.

As my brother and sister-in-law were also going to the lunch, I'd arranged to meet them beforehand, so we could have coffee together. From there I was to travel on to Coventry Cathedral to record a broadcast. Yes, the day was going to be full, but because I'd planned it well, it was perfectly feasible to fit everything in. That was until things started to go wrong.

The car wouldn't start and I had to get the breakdown service out. Thoughts of early morning shopping were abandoned. Because the battery had gone flat, the car radio would no longer function. So, as I travelled along, I had to sing to myself – not a pleasant experience. When I got to a village supermarket, I discovered that I'd left my shopping list behind. I then had difficulty finding my brother – the place at which I'd suggested we meet didn't exist! Thank God for mobile phones (something I never thought I'd say). The final straw was when I put my dog collar on and the stud broke. That was all I needed.

Now when that sort of thing happens to some people, they believe that God has got it in for them. I don't. I just think it's a great nuisance to be overcome. If I need help, I'll ask for it. We don't live in a world where everything goes the way we want it to, so we shouldn't be surprised when it doesn't. Don't let it get you down. It's probably so trivial that it's not worth getting worked up about. How you cope will depend on your attitude. Be positive.

7

Peace and Quiet

In the previous chapter I mentioned that Jesus seemed to take storms in his stride. He slept through them. The scene is the Sea of Galilee at the end of what had been a very full day. To get away from the crowds, Jesus suggested that he and the disciples should get into a boat and go across to the other side. As can happen on the Sea of Galilee, a sudden storm arose, whipping up the waves. The boat Jesus was in started taking in water. The disciples didn't hesitate to wake the sleeping Jesus: '"Teacher, do you not care if we perish?" And he awoke and rebuked the wind and the sea, "Peace! Be still!" And the wind ceased and there was a great calm.'

There was another time when Jesus calmed a storm. But this time it wasn't a physical one. There were no winds or waves. It was a storm of the mind; a storm of the heart. This time the scene is an upper room in Jerusalem on Easter night. The doors were locked, as were the hearts and minds of those people who were in that room. Through the locked doors came the risen Christ and his message was the one they most wanted to hear: 'Peace be with you.'

The disciples had heard this message once before. It was the night before Jesus was crucified, and again they were all together in an upper room. According to St John's Gospel, Jesus used the opportunity to give his disciples some special tuition, which he hoped would sustain them through the coming hours. He promised them peace. 'Peace I leave with you; my peace I give to you; not as the world gives do I give. Let not your hearts be troubled, neither let them be afraid.'

I have a pet theory about 'The Peace' given during the Communion Service. The more indifferent a congregation is to visitors or even regulars after the service, the more enthusiastic they are for The Peace during the service! But this may just be me being cynical!

Hand in hand with peace goes quiet; an inner quiet, from which strength can be drawn. In even the most crowded situations, it is possible to create an oasis of quiet, but only if there is peace at the centre of your own heart.

Through the scrapyard

Not far from Exeter, set in the heart of the glorious Devon countryside, there's a wonderful retreat house. It's a place where people go to recharge their spiritual and physical batteries, surrounded by beauty. As far as the eye can see there are fields, trees, hedgerows and a river. However, there's one drawback.

When I first visited the site, I turned off the winding valley road, crossed a bridge and then started my ascent up a small lane. Suddenly, amid all this loveliness, I was confronted by a scrapyard. Tangled bits of metal, rusting parts of engines and redundant steel girders were all piled high in an unsightly mess. I couldn't get past quickly enough. My sights were set on the retreat house at the end of the lane and I certainly didn't want to be distracted by all this muck, chaos and confusion.

But I was being rather unrealistic because in life you often have to go through the garbage to get to the glory. Certainly, if you want to be more like Christ, you've got to root out all the unsightly traits in your own character before you stand even the remotest chance of aspiring to perfection.

Take a look at the saints. You'll find that first they had to deal with weaknesses within themselves before they could be recognized for their spiritual greatness. If I understand correctly, we all have to pass through a spiritual scrapyard before there can be any hope of moral or spiritual growth.

Sins such as jealousy, greed, lying and envy are never very attractive, and unless they're scrapped, they can dominate our lives. They will govern our attitude to others, and we'll deny ourselves any hope of being at peace with ourselves, and so being at peace with God.

Beating a retreat

I don't know where you're planning to go on your next holiday, but if you're keen on walking, I can certainly recommend Abergavenny on the Welsh Borders. I know it's a long way to go if you're reading this in Australia, but I can assure you that you won't be disappointed.

Abergavenny used to be my bolt-hole, a most welcoming retreat. Whenever life got too much for me in London and I was fed up with the filthy fumes, I'd pack my walking boots, get into my car and head west. Just the sight of the Black Mountains and the Brecon Beacons restored my enthusiasm for life, and after only a couple of days I felt I could face London's Elephant and Castle once again.

Sadly, my cover was blown after I presented the BBC's *Songs of Praise* from there, so I've had to find somewhere else. And I'm not telling you where it is!

I'm not the first person to need a safe haven. Elijah certainly did. It wasn't the fumes of Jerusalem getting up his nose nor the stress of modern living: it was woman trouble. If ever a devil was born without horns, it was Jezebel.

She was a terrible thorn in Elijah's side. Not only was his one God more effective than all her gods put together, but Elijah also disapproved of her greed and had the courage to tell her so. No wonder he had to get away!

However, it wasn't long before he was back to face the fray. And that's exactly what retreats are for – places where you can go to take stock, lick wounds and recharge your batteries.

You don't necessarily have to travel. You may have a quiet room in your own home or a favourite corner of the garden. If not, how about the local park or an unlocked church? You could even plug in your personal stereo and lose yourself in Mozart, Manilow or Madonna. Music makes a very effective sanctuary.

There's no need to think that by retreating to your bolt-hole you're running away. You're simply stepping aside for a while, so you can return to life restored and refreshed.

Quality time

Every so often we're hit by new phrases. 'Quality time' is certainly one of them. It has come to describe that time when, free from worry or pressure, we can do something really worth while.

A couple of months ago, the grandmother of one of my Godchildren died. But before she did so, David had been able to spend time just being with her. He was able to say his 'goodbye' properly, and that could definitely be described as 'quality time'.

Sitting down with children when they return from school is quality time. Nearly always they're bubbling over with all they've done during the day and are longing for you to listen. Those few minutes spent together are precious. You'll soon come to learn how special they are when, only a few years later, you're lucky if you can get a word out of your children about what they've done, where they've been or who they've been with. All children go through the grunting stage, so hang on – the quality time will return!

The family meal is excellent quality time. Sitting down together, listening to one another, enjoying each other's company creates a unique sort of atmosphere. The gradual disappearance of the family meal has done so much damage to our society. Some parents haven't a clue what their children are up to and some children have very little respect for their parents. And all because they never spend quality time together.

The period after the children have gone to bed, when the working day is over and you've a while to relax with the person you love, can also be quality time. But it will depend on how you use it. If you use it to get things off your chest, then you may be minutes away from a row. If, however, you use it to express your love for each other, then that's real quality time.

The time Jesus spent with his closest disciples was, I believe, 'quality time'. It wasn't always easy. On occasions there were difficult things that had to be said, but the atmosphere was right in which to say them. Properly used, prayer time is also quality time. It's the opportunity, before God, to put your life into perspective. You can be truly sorry for the mistakes, grateful for the gifts and supported for the tasks that lie ahead. Quality time, indeed.

Downshifting

Every so often a new word appears. The latest one to come my way is 'downshifting'. This, apparently, is when you decide to take a less prestigious job, a house with fewer bedrooms and a smaller car. Pre-cooked meals are a thing of the past. Fruit and veg become a prominent part of your daily diet. Regular exercise is taken seriously. Yes, everything points to the fact that you're turning your back on today's pressured, competitive society and adopting 'the good life'.

Every time I use my food processor, I realize there's a lot to be said for the simple life. It takes so long to wash up all the bits and pieces, I wonder why on earth I didn't just use a hand-whisk.

Still, the person who decides to downshift turns their back on all these gadgets. Life is for living rather than enduring. And I have to say they have my sympathy – although, to be honest, I would hate to be without the telephone or the microwave.

I used to visit some nuns who lived just off junction 7 of the M4. Their lifestyle couldn't have been simpler. Their day was dedicated to prayer and domestic work, and talking was kept to a minimum. On major feast days, such as Christmas and Easter, they invited people to tea. It was a simple meal, the only hint of luxury being a tin of sweets they'd been given and this, of course, they would share with their guests. With their lifestyle it would have been pretty difficult to downshift, which is probably why their community radiated a sense of tranquillity.

We really do clutter up our lives, often making them far more complicated than we need to. A really good clear-out is what's called for. Get rid of all the clutter and just focus on the essentials. You may not impress the neighbours but you'll enjoy a better life!

Once more with feeling

'Again! Again!' I'd already played pat-a-cake three times but four-year-old Barbara wanted the fun to continue. So I tried something different. I put out my hand. She put one hand on top, then I put my other hand on top and she put hers on top of that ...

Within seconds our hands were in a great jumble and Barbara was in fits of laughter. 'Again!' she cried.

My two-year-old nephew Tomás preferred something a little more energetic. Sitting astride my ankle, supported by my foot, he wanted to be bounced up and down to 'Ride a Cock-horse to Banbury Cross'. Tomás is no lightweight. After two goes, Uncle Roger was beginning to reveal signs of strain. Was Tomás prepared to show understanding and sympathy? Was he heck! 'Again! Again!' he cried.

Although minutes away from collapse, I obliged. Fortunately, despite more cries of 'Again!' Tomás' parents came to my rescue. 'Tomás, leave poor old Uncle Roger alone.' Tomás was removed from my ankle and I went into a sulk at being called 'old'!

At what age do children learn the word 'again'? It's certainly very early and, what's more, they know exactly what it means. When the going is good, they don't want it to stop. Not unlike adults. The only difference is that they're honest enough to say so.

However, none of us can expect fun 24 hours a day, seven days a week. As well as happiness in life, there's often sadness. This isn't an easy lesson to learn and for children it can be quite bewildering. But then adults aren't always able to cope with setbacks, disappointment or failure either.

Jesus alerted his disciples to the fact that life wasn't going to be a bed of roses for them. St Paul often warned the newly converted Christians that sorrow could still lie ahead. Conversion didn't automatically lead to non-stop delight.

We've every right to enjoy the happiness that comes our way. But it's the manner in which we handle sorrow that shows our real worth.

Coming clean

'No one's going out to play until someone owns up.' How those words, which I first heard in school 50 years ago, still ring in my ears! They usually meant that someone had broken a chair, made an unseemly noise, written something on the blackboard or spilt ink on the floor. And they were always followed by total silence, which became increasingly uneasy as time went on.

When it looked as if not only playtime would disappear, but also that the end of the school day might be delayed, the silence became very uncomfortable indeed. As we sat there, straight backed and arms folded, furtive glances were passed around the class until someone broke.

At first, there would be a vague response on the lines of 'Miss, I think it was an accident. It just sort of happened.'

Finally, after further enquiries and long pauses, the guilty person would be exposed, sentence would be passed and the rest of us allowed to go. But what a business! The recriminations in the playground went on for the rest of the day and all because no one was prepared to come clean and own up.

It's a scene re-enacted every day, the world over, and not only in school. Adults can be as reluctant as children to admit their mistakes. The first human story in the Bible involves this very subject. Adam and Eve found it extremely difficult to acknowledge their wrongdoing.

Indeed, this theme dominates the Bible until Jesus appears on the scene. By dying on the Cross, he was prepared to own up not just for himself but for everyone.

Coming clean is a sign of strength. It shows we can take responsibility for our actions and face the consequences. What's more, having learnt from our experiences, we're given the chance to start again. So, go on, come clean with God, yourself and those you love.

Behind locked doors

One day I nipped out of the house, only for an hour, but in my haste I forgot to double-lock the front door. When I returned I found my home had been broken into. They had taken my TV and video, which were easily replaced. They had also taken some chairs and little pieces of silver, most of which were irreplaceable.

Until then, I'd never been very security conscious. Living in a small terraced house, I'd thought I was safe, but now I have extra bolts on the door and locks on the windows. I even have a chain on the front door (though, stupidly, I don't use it). It's not quite Fort Knox but it's not far off.

However, my security arrangements are nothing compared to the precautions that were taken by the 11 disciples on that first Easter Day. They knew that, apart from John, they had all let Jesus down. And now they were leaderless, uncertain what the future held, living behind locked doors. According to St John's Gospel, the doors were locked because of their fear of the Jews, but I'm not so sure. They may have been frightened of the Jews but I think they were more frightened of themselves.

When people are very frightened they often lock themselves away, if not physically then metaphorically. Caught in the grip of fear, they cut themselves off, even from those who might be able to help.

However, the locked doors were no barrier to the risen Jesus. He came through them and forced the disciples to face up to their fear. His message was, 'Peace be with you,' and this eventually overcame their fear and gave them the peace and freedom they needed to get out.

Those of you who live in fear need to hear the Easter message of peace. Then you too will be able to unlock your hearts and minds and free yourself of the fear that is dominating, if not ruining, your lives. It's not locks you need, it's freedom, and that only comes through a sense of peace.

Wrong to be right

If you're ever short of a pithy saying, turn to the Book of Proverbs in the Old Testament. It's a goldmine.

Take this one: 'A fool thinks he is always right; wise is the man who listens to advice.' And of course, what's true for a man is also true for women.

Some people can't bear to be in the wrong. The subject or the situation doesn't matter, what they say goes and heaven help anyone who tries to disagree with them. Their arrogance knows no bounds. They're impossible to work for and extremely difficult to live with. However, getting them to see the error of their ways is well-nigh impossible.

When you find this in a child, you realize that they know no better. But when an adult always has to be right, then something is terribly wrong.

St Paul, I believe, was such a person. Being both a Roman citizen and a Pharisee, he was adamant in his opinions. No wonder he was willing to guard the coats of those who stoned Stephen to death. This new faith Stephen was preaching had to be wrong. After all, it didn't accord with Paul's beliefs.

It took a blinding experience on the road to Damascus to bring Paul to his senses. But even then he didn't find it very easy to accept being in the wrong. Nor did St Peter. Hence the clashes between them as they tried to establish the new Christian church.

Such conflicts will always occur if people aren't prepared to listen or take advice. And this is as true between nations as it is between husband and wife, parent and child, or between friends. No relationship is going to last if one party has always got to be right.

There's a vital ingredient missing in the person who won't brook contradiction, and that's humility. Humility is essential if you are to accept any advice. It's only the arrogant who think that they know everything.

Panic attack!

She was already looking harassed, as though her journey to the station had been fraught. Then, having checked several times that she was boarding the right train, this lady, probably in her mid- to late-60s, was faced with the problem of her luggage. Being a former Cub, I came to her rescue. With her large suitcase safely on the rack, she settled herself into her seat.

About halfway through the journey she decided it was time for a snack, so she made her way to the buffet car. It was then that her panic attack began. She couldn't remember where she'd been sitting. As every carriage tends to look the same, it's a mistake anyone can make.

After she'd passed me twice, once in each direction, I thought it was time I intervened. I went after her and escorted her safely back to her seat.

The expression on her face said it all. She couldn't have been more grateful. For the rest of the journey she remained firmly where she was.

I did sympathize with her. I've had similar panics when I've mislaid a credit card, or shut the front door before checking I've got the key, or left the house wondering whether I've turned off the iron. Some panic attacks can be avoided if you take a little more time over what you're doing but some are unavoidable.

If it's someone else who's panicking, then help them in a calm and practical way. Don't add to their burden, relieve it. And if it's you who's suffering, why not turn to others? It's certainly one way to ease the tension, though sadly, many people are too proud to ask for help.

Alternatively, you could turn to God. Prayer, at times of panic, introduces a sense of calm and stillness to your agitated mind and helps to put matters in perspective. Panic produces more panic, whereas prayer produces peace.

Building up power

Yet again my train from Manchester arrived late. This time it was due to 'a loss of power in the Bletchley area'. This reminded me of how easy it is for humans to lose power. I know just what it's like to feel tired and come to a complete standstill.

There's an interesting story in the Gospels about power, in between the two parts of the story of the healing of Jairus' daughter. Jesus was on his way to Jairus' house when a woman who had suffered haemorrhages for 12 years heard that he was due to pass by. He was her last resort. There wasn't a doctor she hadn't consulted, but no one had been able to relieve her ordeal.

As she made her way through the crowd she realized she wouldn't be able to speak to Jesus, but she reckoned that if she could just touch his clothes she'd be healed. And as she touched them, so Jesus felt power go out of him.

We all know how exhausting it can be caring for others. The demands of our own lives are great enough, but with the added responsibility of someone else there are times when we feel quite exhausted. The problem is, how do we recharge our batteries and regain power?

First of all we have to acknowledge we've come to a full stop: people only damage themselves when they are too proud to admit they are at the end of their strength. And then, having faced the truth, we need to get help – not always easy but not impossible either. It's often only our own stubbornness that keeps us from it.

Having got help, we must let someone else do the worrying while we rest, renew our strength and get things into perspective. Very soon we'll be firing on all cylinders again.

For his power, Jesus always turned to his Father in prayer. Let's follow his example, because from prayer comes real power, something that's not easily drained.

Say it with meaning

I have to confess I don't always do what I'm told on an aircraft. But then how many of us ever listen properly to the safety regulations before takeoff?

However, I was forced to think again during a recent flight from Belfast when we were asked to pay attention to safety instructions, which would be demonstrated for us by 'Bert, Matilda and Flopsy'. Suddenly everyone on the plane sat up and took note. Hardened businessmen lowered their newspapers, power-dressed women closed their files and even parents told their young children to be quiet and listen.

It's amazing what a change of routine can achieve. And what's true of safety instructions on an aircraft is certainly true of prayer. The Lord's Prayer rattled off at top speed in a meaningless manner is of little use. Yet that's what so often happens. 'Let's get it over and done with' seems to be the motivation, and those who lead worship can be just as guilty as the people in the pews. It's no wonder that many give up on God when the means of keeping in touch with him is gabbled garbage.

The problem is far from new. Jesus, in the Sermon on the Mount, having told his listeners not to make a public show of their prayers, gives them a piece of sound advice: 'In your prayers do not go babbling on like the heathen who imagine the more they say, the more likely they are to be heard.'

He then goes on to teach them how to pray. This is where the Lord's Prayer comes in. Jesus offers it to his listeners as a pattern for prayer, not as a mechanical formula to be trotted out on every occasion. When it's used as a pattern, it's powerful. Broken down section by section, it covers all the situations of everyday life.

Any prayer will lose its edge if it degenerates into vain repetition. Rattling off a routine will fall on deaf ears. For prayer to be powerful at all, it must have meaning and it must be sincere.

Naming the hall

I've no idea how Prince Albert felt when the famous concert hall was named after him. Nor do I know what Sir John Gielgud thought when his name appeared over the theatre in Shaftesbury Avenue. But I do know how Mrs Pat Oxlade felt when Dorney County Primary School named their new school hall after her. She was over the moon. She felt both proud and humble.

Pat Oxlade isn't a local dignitary, a former headteacher, or even an international superstar. She was the school's cleaner and had been working there since 1955. She officially retired last year after 40 years' service, but she's still very much a presence in Dorney School. What Pat has shown is that in service there is dignity.

Isaiah prophesied that the Messiah would be the 'Suffering Servant', and when Jesus was born he fulfilled that prophecy. To his disciples, as well as being their leader he was also their servant. He actually said to them, 'I am among you as one who serves,' and at the Last Supper he took a towel and washed the disciples' feet to show them that, as he wasn't above doing such things, nor should his followers be.

Somehow in this country we have degraded the idea of service. Servants are looked down upon or ignored yet without a sense of service, life would come to a standstill.

Pat Oxlade, as well as maintaining the highest standards of cleanliness, became a good friend to staff, governors, children and their families. She always supported the school beyond the call of duty, by making teas and coffees or serving at jumble sales, concerts, sports days, fêtes and parents' meetings. She's a peaceful person who never sought the limelight but got on with her job quietly and never to the exclusion of other people.

The real servant is one who knows her or his own value and yet is more than ready to value other people. Making life easier for others brings great joy. There can be nothing finer than being a good and faithful servant, because through that sort of service comes perfect freedom. I felt very honoured to be asked to open the Oxlade Hall because here was service being given the recognition it deserved.

Plumping up the cushions

I shall never forget one of my first funeral visits as a young curate in Portsmouth. It was to the home of an elderly couple where the husband had died the day before. The widow didn't come to church but she still made me very welcome. I was shown into the front room – a room, I believe, that was only used on high days and holy days and, of course, for entertaining visiting clergy. It was late in the afternoon, I'd had a demanding day and, as I listened to the widow's gentle voice as it wafted through a forest of aspidistras, I nodded off to sleep. The next thing I knew it was about an hour later and I was being offered a cup of tea. I was very embarrassed and full of apologies but the widow couldn't have been more understanding. 'I was pleased you felt so relaxed and comfortable in my home,' she said. What a lovely lady, I thought. She so easily could have been offended but in fact she was exactly the opposite.

There have been other homes I've visited where, despite the outward show of comfort, I've felt anything but comfortable. I've had to be very careful about the chair I chose in case I was usurping somebody's place. Every time I stood up, I had to plump the cushions so as not to leave even the slightest impression that I'd been there. There was certainly no chance of my dropping off to sleep on those occasions. I spent most of the time watching my Ps and Qs.

Jesus far preferred the company of publicans and sinners to that of the so-called righteous of his day. The righteous thought they were doing Jesus a favour by having him in their house. The publicans and sinners thought exactly the opposite. They were indeed privileged to have Jesus with them and so they went out of their way to make him feel welcome.

Over the years I've depended on the hospitality of others and I've been very grateful to those who've made me so welcome in their homes. Now that I'm able to return the compliment I hope people coming to my home feel welcome and wanted. There's nothing worse than finding a welcome mat at the door but no genuine welcome inside. Stop worrying about the plumped-up cushions. Every host should feel that things have gone well when their guests leave with a good impression.

8

Tears and Sorrow

It's the shortest verse in the Bible and yet for many the most telling: 'Jesus wept.' The home at Bethany of Martha, Mary and their brother Lazarus was obviously somewhere special for Jesus. He could relax, be himself and enjoy the company of personal friends. So naturally the human Jesus was sad when he saw Lazarus dead and the home in mourning. No one wants to be separated from someone they love. The divine Jesus had no worries. He seized the opportunity to let his friends in on a truth that was yet to be revealed: 'I am the resurrection and the life.' Tears and sorrow can lead to hope and fulfilment.

This was not, however, the only time that Jesus was in tears. On another occasion it was for a place and its people. It was Jerusalem. For Jesus, his first real glimpse of the city would have been as he approached the summit of the Mount of Olives. Seeing the city filled his heart with sadness and his eyes with tears. Here was a city that had everything and yet . . . It had failed to reach its potential. It had destroyed those who had tried to show it the error of its ways and it was about to miss yet another opportunity. It failed to recognize the Messiah in its midst. All the future held for that city was destruction. This made Jesus not angry, but very sad.

The next time Jesus is associated with tears, the tears are not his. They are Peter's. This highly trusted disciple has let Jesus down. He has denied him, at a time when Jesus needed him most. It took just one look and Peter 'went out and wept bitterly'.

Tears aren't always brought on by other people. They are often brought on by ourselves. We fail to achieve those standards God expects of us and in sorrow we weep. These tears, though, can be refreshing. They are the outward sign that we accept our failure and have taken the first step towards repentance and regeneration.

We should never be frightened of tears. The stiff upper lip philosophy has done immense long-term damage. Tears are held back. Emotions are not expressed. So instead of having the courage to be our real selves, we put on an act, trying to be people we are not and have never wanted to be.

Like all water, tears refresh. They are the natural way of allowing yourself to face sorrow and then, hopefully, overcome it.

Hidden pain

Broken legs can be set in plaster. And broken arms can be cradled in a sling. You can even wrap a bandage round a grazed knee. But how do you mend a broken heart?

There won't often be any obvious physical symptoms to be treated, but there will be a deep hidden pain that shouldn't be ignored. One of the privileges of being a priest is that people trust me with secrets that they have never revealed to anyone but God, and sometimes not even to him.

With older people, that secret could be that they were born out of wedlock and still suffer shame. It may be a parent who has lost contact with a child, or someone who appears to be a widow but, in reality, is divorced.

Feelings stretching back over the years, along with deep-seated guilt, can be a great source of anguish, though this is often masked by a brave face. But just as physical damage can cause permanent harm if it's ignored, so can inner hurt. Then the brave face can be twisted into torment.

The only way to cope with hidden pain is to uncover it, to bring it into the air. One of the best ways to do this is to expose it to prayer, so that rather than hugging it to yourself you can share it with God. The relief may not be immediate but praying is an excellent way to put things into perspective and start the process of healing.

It also helps if you can share your distress with someone you really trust. Gradually the pain will ease and you will be able to begin to rebuild your life without the burden of the past. You can then look forward with hope, rather than back with regret.

Life to the full

My mother died of a massive stroke. It happened on a Monday evening and she was dead by midday Tuesday. Obviously the last thing I wanted was for her to die, and her death threw my life into turmoil.

But had she lived, the quality of her life would have been almost non-existent. So I was very pleased that the doctors and nurses made her comfortable but didn't connect her to machines for the sake of keeping the body alive, knowing full well that the mind had gone. Nor did they give my brother or myself the agonizing decision of when the machines should be turned off. My mother died in peace and at peace.

That was more than 40 years ago. Medicine has come a long way since then. Now doctors, relatives and even patients are faced with some desperate dilemmas. Although I know the word euthanasia means 'good death', I don't believe it can ever be justified, even when it is claimed to be voluntary. To me life is sacred. This doesn't mean that physical life should be kept going at all costs, but it does mean that it should not be deliberately destroyed.

Although people accuse the hospice movement of hypocrisy, I feel its philosophy is right. The possibility of death is not ignored. It's properly prepared for by both the patient and the family. Pain is kept to a minimum and, if treatment eventually leads to death, then so be it.

As with the abortion debate, there will be people with strongly held views on both sides. However, as we have seen with abortion, when permission is given to take life, a hornets' nest is disturbed. Loophole after loophole is found by those who want to take the law into their own hands. And something that was intended to relieve distress becomes an absolute minefield.

Suffering for suffering's sake is pointless, but when the person is cared for properly, it can bring inner strength both to the sufferer and those who support him or her. Whereas killing someone can only bring guilt, and that can be so destructive.

Tale of rejection

Try as I might, I can't get into opera. The long arias and interminable death scenes are not my cup of tea. It also doesn't help that at some venues you need to take out an extra mortgage to pay for your seat! However, recently a friend invited me to see *Madam Butterfly* at the London Coliseum. Being someone who never overlooks an invitation or a night out, I accepted. And on the whole, I'm extremely glad I did.

The production was brilliant and the singer who played Butterfly had the voice of an angel. But I didn't leave the theatre with a spring in my step or humming any of the tunes. On the contrary, as I made my way to the bus stop I felt rather battered and bruised. The story of Madam Butterfly herself is far from being a giggle a minute.

This tale of loyalty and rejection takes place before the First World War, when a US Marine, Pinkerton, marries a young geisha girl. For him it's just a casual affair, since he knows that in Japanese law the absence of a husband for as little as a month can constitute a divorce. For her, it's a lifetime's commitment. When his ship sails, Butterfly, confident that he'll be back, brings up his child and awaits his return. But when Pinkerton does come back to Japan he brings an American wife with him.

Butterfly's life is completely shattered. She feels she has nothing to live for any more. Having taken a last farewell of her son, who is now to live with his father, she kills herself.

After a story like that, it's hardly surprising I felt down as I left the theatre. But sadly, feelings of rejection and tested loyalty are all too common. Indeed, they're at the heart of the Christian faith. Both in the Garden of Gethsemane and on the Cross, Jesus experiences rejection, and not just by his closest friends. He even feels that his heavenly Father has rejected him. 'My God, my God, why have you forsaken me?' he cries. However, Jesus endures, and with the dawn of Easter Day the rejection is turned into acceptance and the loyalty is renewed.

Rejection is a powerfully destructive force. It's painful to be told you're not wanted and no longer of any use. And yet it's something we all experience in one way or another. The most important thing is to have the strength to live through it. I firmly believe that after the crucifixion must come the resurrection.

Drowning your sorrows

Cans of drink at the corner shop, bottles of wine at the supermarket and longer opening hours at the pub have all made alcohol more readily available. And it's causing a problem. In no way do I want to underestimate the destructiveness of drugs, but I do think we're being hypocritical if we stress this while ignoring the ever-increasing damage caused by drink. And I don't just mean on the roads. Several of my friends have had their lives ruined by drink, and only a few weeks ago I received a letter signed 'Simon's mother, a *Woman's Weekly* reader', telling me how the writer's son had lost his job, his home and his marriage because of drink.

Alcoholics are sick people. Often they start by drowning their sorrows but soon they're drowning in the drink that was meant to console them. And until they're able to admit the problem to themselves, there's not the slightest chance of their ever being able to cope with it.

Some people avoid alcohol at all costs. The Salvation Army, as well as many strict Methodists and Baptists, is set against it, but it certainly isn't banned in the Bible. Jesus' first miracle was to turn water into wine at the wedding at Cana in Galilee, and we're encouraged to 'take a little wine for thy stomach's sake'. But as with all gifts, it needs to be used properly.

Children need to be educated in the ways of drinking. 'Alcopops' are a curse and I'm very pleased the trade is now taking them, and the effect they can have on the young, seriously. A child needs to learn about drinking at the family meal table. Obviously, any parent who gives a child spirits is irresponsible. But a little wine with a meal can add to the enjoyment without rendering the person incapable or destroying the brain cells. Wine isn't then seen as something illicit, but is enjoyed as it should be – with food and in moderation.

I've nothing but respect for the work of Alcoholics Anonymous. They've helped people rebuild lives that have been devastated by drink. Their service is totally confidential and their motto is 'One day at a time'. Obedience to that motto is what it takes to recover from a life dominated by drink. Some people are more susceptible to the dangers of drink than others, but all of us need to be aware that big trouble can be born from small beginnings. Whatever you do, never give a drink to someone who says 'No'.

Unsolved problems

Far be it from me to try and do Mary Marryat's job for her, but as this letter came to me from a reader, I thought I'd have a go at answering it. She's a very caring daughter whose mother, who is in her late 70s, is slowly destroying herself.

The mother has just one brother, now a widower, and the two of them were extremely close when they were young. They went everywhere together and were the best of friends. They both married and had families and lived near enough to each other to spend every Christmas, Easter, summer holiday, birthday, and so on, together.

Then, in their 60s, they had a silly row and instead of just putting it behind them, the brother became quite vindictive. He'll have nothing to do with his sister now. He returns birthday and Christmas cards unopened and puts the phone down if she tries to ring him. They haven't spoken for nearly 15 years.

All this is eating into the sister. She has really tried to make amends and, even though she realizes that they'll probably never be the best of friends again, she'd like to repair the damage and make up before she goes to her grave. She's frightened of dying with it hanging over her.

This sort of situation is more common than you might think. It's also more destructive than cancer because it really can destroy the soul. In the Sermon on the Mount, Jesus warned his listeners about the dangers of falling out with other people. It can so easily get out of hand. Before you know it you're at daggers drawn and arbitration is a distant hope. Fearing such a situation, St Paul strongly advised the people of Ephesus that they 'should not let the sun go down upon their anger'. Quarrels must be made up or they become all-out war.

However, this is easier said than done. It takes two to quarrel. It also takes two to make it up. It looks as though this sister has done everything she can to bring about healing but her brother simply won't budge. So in no way should she feel guilty.

May I suggest that someone acts as a go-between? The brother may not realize the hell he's creating. I think someone needs to point this out to him. The opportunity for a new start is one that shouldn't be ignored, particularly when it comes to families and friendship.

Tongue twister

I've never believed the saying, 'Sticks and stones may break my bones but words will never hurt me.' On the contrary, I favour, 'Gossip can be sharp as a sword but the tongue of the wise heals.'

It's often much easier to cope with physical pain than mental torture. An unkind or careless word can leave a far deeper scar than any bodily injury, and it takes a lot longer to heal.

Gossip is so destructive. Though generally based on half-truths, misinformation and petty jealousy, once it's up and running there's no stopping it. As it gathers momentum, details are added. What was rumour becomes fact. And until someone has the courage to confront the victim of the gossip, a pack of lies is passed off as Gospel truth.

The Ten Commandments are perfectly clear. They may not mention the word 'gossip' but they certainly rule out 'false witness', and that's what gossip usually is. St James, in what must be one of the most practical of all the Epistles, tells the early Christians to watch their tongues. As he says, 'It is a small member but it can make huge claims'. So he advises them to use their tongues wisely, as gossip should play no part in their lives. We are all attracted to gossip. We all like to be in the know. It's only when we are the subject of gossip we come to realize how harmful it can be.

The same is true about the cutting remarks we make. Some of us are far too clever with our tongues for our own good, let alone the goodness of others.

How much better it is to have a tongue that heals, that only passes on what it knows to be the truth, that encourages people rather than belittles them, that remains silent if it has nothing positive to say. If you train your tongue in this way, not only will you gain the respect of others, you'll also find it easier to live with yourself.

Give it a go!

There can hardly be a single activity, age group or hobby for which there isn't a magazine. Newsagents' shelves are stacked high and the choice can be quite bewildering.

Nowadays there are lots of new magazines on the scene, as well as tabloid newspapers, chock-a-block with celebrities caught off guard. Glamour girls without their make-up, or household names having rows in public, famous faces looking down in the mouth. These are their staple diet. They're a great money spinner for the paparazzi but it must be very depressing for those whose photos are taken. However glamorous you are, there are bound to be times when you feel anything but. Even the happiest person isn't protected from sadness.

Why should anyone want to produce such publications, let alone buy them? It's because so many people have a nasty streak. They far prefer to see others at their weakest and most vulnerable, so they can gloat. After all, other people's failings are always a lot more interesting than our own.

There is something wrong with this attitude. Although many people spent their time finding fault with Jesus, he always looked for the good in people. Jesus was able to detect a spark of goodness in even the greatest sinner and was prepared to nurture it until it became a flame. He taught his disciples to do the same.

It's easy to criticize and condemn, and yet it's more positive to praise and encourage. It's a ground rule for good teaching. Children flourish and bloom when encouraged, so why, when we become adults, do we prefer to tear people apart rather than build them up? We hate it when it happens to us and yet we're prepared to do it to others.

It would stop if we started to appreciate, admire and encourage the good in everybody's life. It would be a better idea if we encouraged the goodness in our own lives, because that would encourage us to look for the goodness in others. Go on – for goodness' sake, give it a go.

Rules and regulations

For the bride, this was her third marriage. Her first was annulled; her second ended with the tragic death of her husband. For the groom, it was his second marriage. His first had ended in divorce after 16 years and two children. The wedding ceremony was a low-key civil one, and yet the Pope had seen it necessary to give a special dispensation to the couple because one was a Roman Catholic and the other a Protestant. Why this was necessary God only knows. It could be because this was no ordinary couple. The bride was Princess Caroline of Monaco, the groom Prince Ernst of Hanover.

The Church, and it doesn't matter which denomination we're talking about, gets itself into a muddle when it starts to play about with its own man-made rules and regulations. I've never been sure of the grounds for an annulment. Obviously non-consummation must be one, but after that the grounds become, to me, confused. For instance, does it help if you have money, position or influence? Or am I just being a little cynical? I really don't know.

Churches have got themselves into a real mess when dealing with marriage. There's no doubt whatsoever what the ideal is. Marriage is for better for worse, for richer, for poorer, in sickness and in health, until death – and it is the churches' job to uphold that ideal. But many people, even with the best of intentions, fall short of it. Should they be cast out? I think not.

Over the years, I've come to realize the pain caused by divorce to all sides and especially to children. I don't believe it's the churches' task to condemn them. They must be able to offer hope and healing. This will not come about through annulments or dispensations for the few. It will only happen when the churches have the courage to come out from behind their rules and regulations and focus their minds on God's love and forgiveness.

Risky business

A new clause has crept into my house contents insurance policy. It seems that I'm now covered for All Risks.

Whether this also covers Acts of God, I'm not sure, although in my view it's impossible not to take risks where God is concerned. Believing in God is a risk in itself since no one can prove his existence. It's an act of faith and acts of faith don't come with a guarantee.

Certainly, the first disciples took enormous risks when they decided to leave their jobs, their homes and their families to obey Jesus' call to follow him. And having taken that initial leap into the big unknown, their lives became even more insecure. They weren't able to protect themselves with personal possessions, and because they were constantly on the move, they denied themselves the basic reassurance of having a home base. They were certainly not insured against all risks.

However much we may long for security, we have to face the fact that life is full of hazards. The world of employment is riven with uncertainty. Even jobs that at one time were thought to be for life are now far from guaranteed.

Friendship and marriage are fraught with many challenges. The moment you commit yourself to someone you're taking a risk. The relationship could totally transform your life, giving it a dimension you've never dreamed of before. But it could also expose you to rejection and despair. That's the risk you have to take.

Although it's sensible to minimize risk where possible, it's unrealistic to hope to banish it entirely. We can't do it physically, emotionally or spiritually. Risk will be a part of our lives until the day we die. And when that day eventually comes, we face the greatest risk of all and it's one we should make sure we're prepared for.

Looking death in the eye

Far be it from me to criticize the work of Marie Curie Cancer Care. The quality of support provided by its staff is quite outstanding, as I know only too well. Several of my very close friends have been sustained and strengthened by their professional, yet highly personal care.

However, I strongly disagreed with the wording of an advertising campaign on behalf of this excellent organization. On a hoarding near me was a poster promoting Marie Curie Cancer Care. It bears, in very large letters, the startling announcement: NEVER SAY DIE.

Now I find this assertion most misleading. Much as we may not wish to admit it, the time comes when we do have to say 'die'. The important thing is to be able to say it without regret.

Years ago, a lady whom I was visiting in hospital knew that she was dying. She told me so and she wanted to talk to me about it. However, her doctor always side-stepped the issue and her family positively avoided it. In fact they became very cross with me when they discovered that I'd been discussing the subject with her.

Fortunately, by the time I had to conduct their mother's funeral, they'd come round to my way of thinking and were grateful that she had died fully prepared, with no regrets or remorse. Death is something we all have to face and it's very unwise to think that if we don't look it in the eye, it'll go away. It won't.

If we can live every day as though it's our last, when we do come to die, whether it be after a long life or a tragic accident, we'll not be caught out. We'll be properly prepared.

I hope you don't think that I'm being morbid. Obviously, my strong conviction that there is life after death, whatever form it may take, sustains me. However, even if you don't share my belief, being well prepared for death is something that we should all strive for.

'Never say die' may be a fine motto for the fictional James Bond, but for real, thinking people it's merely a trite and meaningless remark.

'I want to hold your hand'

It was a Friday afternoon and the train was packed. People were scrambling for seats and luggage was piled high. Just before the train was due to leave the station, a harassed young mother appeared in the compartment. Weighed down with buggies and bags, toys and teddies, she was carrying one child while the other one tried to keep up. Suddenly there was a look of panic on the little girl's face. She clearly feared that she'd lose sight of her mother in the crowd. From this tiny person came a very big plea, 'Mummy, I want to hold your hand!'

How some young mothers manage I'll never know. They get on and off buses and trains with more things than I'd risk carrying even with the aid of a pick-up truck. They often have to keep a vigilant eye on a child in tow who, in turn, dreads losing sight of their mother, as I remember so well from my own experience.

All of us face times when we're frightened. We're on our own, we don't know which way to go, we're lost. The one thing we'd love to be able to say, whatever age we are, is, 'Mummy, I want to hold your hand.'

The moment that little girl grabbed hold of her mother's hand, the look of panic disappeared from her face. Don't we all recognize that feeling? Once we realize that someone is sharing our problem or is there to support us, then the fear goes from our souls and we're able to face the future.

All of us need to know someone to whom we can say, 'I want to hold your hand.' It is, I believe, one of the main characteristics of prayer. When we pray we're saying to God, 'I want to hold your hand.' It demands trust on our part but in return we'll receive the confidence and security essential for a full life.

Great expectations

At 8.08 a.m. I was waiting on Platform 4 of Milton Keynes station for the 8.20 a.m. to London Euston. Across the track on Platform 5 was a couple with their two very young children waiting for the 8.09 a.m. to Preston.

Suddenly the voice of the station announcer sprang to life: 'I am sorry to tell those people waiting on Platform 5 that the 8.09 a.m. train to Preston has been cancelled due to engineering works in the Preston area.'

Across the tracks I could see the faces of the children's parents drop. It was a Saturday morning. Goodness knows what time they'd been up, and getting two children ready for a journey is no easy task. Dejectedly they picked up their children and their luggage and made their way back to the main concourse. What happened to them after that I've no idea.

I really felt for them. So often we get ourselves, and maybe others, all geared up for something special, only to have it come to nothing. Certainly this was no new experience for Moses as he tried to lead the Children of Israel towards the Promised Land. Time and again he was leading them on what he thought was the right track, only to have his plans thwarted. And Jesus' expectations of his disciples were shattered when he found only one of them at the foot of the Cross.

Expectations are part of our lives and there should be great rejoicing when they're fulfilled. But the real test is when they're not fulfilled. Like that young family, doubtless we'll feel downcast. But to stay that way will benefit neither man, woman nor beast. This is the time when we have to pick ourselves up, dust ourselves down and start all over again. Sulking and screaming won't help. Sitting down and thinking through new plans and putting them into action will.

And just as I believe our expectations should be part of our prayers, so should our disappointments. We can learn as much from them, if not more. And very often our disappointments are eventually turned into expectations.

9

Lonely and Alone

In the days when children stood up for adults on buses and smoking was thought to be harmless, there was a brand of cigarette called 'Strand'. Its slogan was, 'You are never alone with a Strand'. The advertising campaign pictured a dejected man, alone, on a dismal London night walking across Waterloo Bridge. From his pocket he took a packet of Strands, lit one and suddenly his mood was transformed. He looked content, at peace with the world and all because he was no longer alone. As the ad said, 'You are never alone with a Strand'. The campaign backfired. Smokers of Strands were eyed with suspicion. They were immediately categorized as sad, lonely people who had to resort to a cigarette for company. The brand was withdrawn.

No one wants to be labelled as lonely. Loneliness is one of the biggest killers in this country. It attacks people, rich and poor, old and young alike. It can be experienced as much in tower blocks as it can on desert islands. It can be felt as much in a crowd as it can on one's own. It is the one thing people dread. Even Christ's disciples needed reassuring that they wouldn't be lonely.

Jesus himself experienced loneliness. In the Garden of Gethsemane, when he could have done with his closest friends at least keeping watch for him, they were fast asleep. Christ's cry of 'My God, my God, why have you forsaken me?' (Psalm 22) from the Cross was a clear indication that Jesus knew the destructive power of loneliness.

However, because of his oneness with his Father he also knew that loneliness can be overcome, and the cry of despair at the start of the Psalm is, in its concluding verses, transformed into a hymn of praise.

He also knew the great difference between being lonely and being alone. Frequently he needed to be alone, to be away from the crowds so as to recharge his spiritual and physical batteries.

It is, after all, when we are alone that we can be aware of the person we are. Stripped of all pomposity and pretence there is no longer the need to put on an act or to play games. It is in these times of aloneness that we are given the power to build on our strengths and to overcome our weaknesses. For in that aloneness Christ is with us, the Christ who said, 'I am with you always until the end of the world.'

The wilderness

Rabbis must be some of the world's greatest storytellers. Certainly Jesus, who was a rabbi, was never short of a good story, and Rabbi Lionel Blue has radio listeners enthralled by his way with words. In a BBC studio, I met Rabbi Dr Jonathan Romain of the Maidenhead Synagogue. I had just come back from my first visit to Jordan. Although my stay was short, I had managed to get to Mount Nebo, the mountain from where Moses is reputed to have seen the Promised Land before he died.

It's an amazing sight. There in front of you lie the wilderness and the Dead Sea, and through the haze you can look towards Bethlehem and Jerusalem. There were not many people about and I just stood in awe and wonder. I told Jonathan about it and in return he told me this very thought-provoking story.

'If we were writing the Bible, it's likely that we would site the giving of the Law to Moses in Jerusalem, which befits the holiest of cities. But God chose to give the Law in the wilderness precisely because it is no man's land, and therefore also every man's land. For the teachings of God are open to all, and no one can claim them exclusively as their own, or declare that they have supremacy over any other people.'

The wilderness can be an empty desert with little or nothing to offer. It can also be a fruitful place. Away from the distractions and demands of everyday life, you can sort out your priorities and delve a little deeper into the things that really matter to you. This Lent, give yourself the space to while away some time in a wilderness. There's no need to go all the way to Jordan. You can create your own private wilderness. You'll be surprised how fertile a wilderness can be.

Going it alone

In the run-up to the millennium, I took a look at the civilizations that shaped the world before the birth of Christ: the Roman civilization, into which Jesus was born, and the Greek civilization, whose power continues to influence many of our ways of thinking, and, of course, the nation that gave birth to civilization itself, Egypt. Strengthened by the waters of the Nile, Egypt set out a way of life that, even today, seems well ahead of its time.

As I stood in wonder at the tombs of kings, one thing struck me. The Egyptian civilization was totally dependent on God – or rather gods.

Even the mighty Rameses II, architect of the temple at Abu Simbel, before he became a god himself, realized his dependence on gods. Offerings were made, prayers were said. Nothing was ventured without seeking their will.

In today's world, God is often the last power to be consulted. After all, who needs God when you have technology? All we have to do is put our minds to it and a solution will be found. In many ways this is wonderful. The advances in medical science have brought relief to countless millions. People living miles apart can be in constant contact.

To belittle or undermine technology is obviously a silly thing to do, but despite our cleverness, I still believe that we're dependent on God. We may not be expected to make the sort of offerings the ancient Egyptians did, but we're still expected to pray. We're still expected to seek out the will of God.

It isn't easy. Nor can we be sure that we've always got it right. However, when we go it alone, we find that instead of creating a more glorious world in which to live, we create weapons of mass destruction, fatal diseases and forces we're unable to control.

Going it alone isn't wise. How much better to go with God, especially at the start of a new millennium.

The reject shop

It's just as well that cups and saucers don't have feelings. I would loathe having 'reject' or 'second' stamped on my bottom. But sadly, that's exactly how some people feel. They believe that because of the way their lot has fallen, they're destined to spend the rest of their lives in the reject shop of life.

With a few people, but only a few, it may be their own fault. They're not prepared to do anything to help themselves or seek support. But for the vast majority, feelings of rejection are caused by the attitude and behaviour of the other people around them.

All minority groups experience these feelings to some extent. Black, Asian, homosexual and disabled people are often made to feel they're 'rejects'. Society may tolerate them, but it doesn't really make them feel at home.

This was exactly how Samaritans, lepers and women felt at the time of Jesus. They were considered second-class citizens along with publicans, tax gatherers and sinners. Rejected by the rest of society, they were forced to live on the fringes. No wonder they were surprised that Jesus had time for them, since no one else ever had. But then Jesus knew all about rejection.

Even within the closeness of a family, it's still possible for one person to feel left out. They may not be as bright as the others or as funny. Their looks may not be quite as stunning or they may not be as easy-going. And so, even if they're not rejected, they feel as though they are, and that's as bad.

Rejection is one of the most damaging human experiences. The rejected child carries the scars through life. The rejected adult is often bewildered. And once rejected, people need a long time to rebuild their confidence. We should always be careful not to reject others.

Behind the mask

I'm a dab hand at breaking glasses, and when it comes to smashing bottles full of coins collected for a good cause, such as The Firemen's Benevolent Fund, I don't mind. Twice now the firefighters of Horton Kirby, Kent, have asked me to come to their local pub to do just that. On the most recent occasion, firefighter Jim came to collect me as usual, but this time he also had someone else to pick up – he wouldn't tell me who.

When we eventually picked up the mystery passenger, I thought I knew the lady. It was the Queen! Of course, it wasn't actually the Queen. It was a lookalike – and a very good one at that. This woman was totally respectful to Her Majesty, and her presence added to what was an enjoyable bit of fun. It was the first time I'd met a double and I was very impressed with the attention to detail.

Later, however, it occurred to me that she wasn't the first lookalike I'd met. Over the years I've come across thousands: people pretending to be what they're not, perhaps wealthier or more influential than they are. I've also met people who claim to be stupid when in fact they're bright. But why? Those who put on an act aren't happy with the way they are. It's extremely sad.

If you hide behind a mask, then no one will get to know the real you. No one, that is, apart from God. For he doesn't look at the outward appearance. He looks at the heart. And the heart is the real person.

Putting on an act is tiring. Sooner or later you'll be found out. The problem then is, what are you left with? Nothing.

By all means change the parts of your character that don't reflect the fact that you're God's child. But make sure the change isn't just cosmetic. Lookalikes are for fun, not for life.

Calling for help

I was thrilled with my new phone. It was cordless, so I could take it with me wherever I went in the house. Life was bliss. Well it was until the thing went wrong. Somehow the base unit had become unplugged, the battery wasn't charging and my contact with the outside world came to a very abrupt halt.

My first reaction was to panic. Then I decided to look for the instruction booklet, which of course I'd put in a 'safe place'. After a three-hour search I found it. There, on the back page, was a helpline number. My problems were over – or so I thought. I rang the number from another phone and was given a whole menu to choose from. I selected the one for cordless phones and then I waited and waited and waited. There was a constant stream of nondescript music interrupted at frequent intervals by a recorded voice, which told me that I was being held in a queue and would be dealt with as soon as an operator became available. After what seemed like an eternity, an operator did become available and I eventually got the help I needed.

I know patience is a virtue, but I also know that it's wrong to offer help and then take a long time to give it. I get very irritated with people who say, 'Now if there's anything I can do, you only have to ask.' Then when you do ask, it's inconvenient.

I know that some people believe that's the way God treats us. However, if we take a more careful look at the way in which Jesus helped people, we shall soon see that he only met their real needs and these didn't always coincide with the needs they thought they had. But nevertheless, help was at hand.

It's useless offering help if you know you're incapable of giving it. You only make matters worse. Before you promise to help, be sure you're up to it. No offer of help is certainly better than a meaningless one.

Hearing aids

Of all the editions of *Songs of Praise* I've presented over the years, there's one that will always stay in my mind.

I was in Falkirk, Scotland. As usual, the church was packed. Choirs had gathered from all over the country and some of them were very unusual indeed.

Because the members were deaf, they were 'signing' choirs. While others sang, they shared in the hymns not with their voices but with their hands and faces. The movements were both graceful and beautiful, conveying the meaning as well as any words.

There was another special ingredient. The researcher working on the programme was profoundly deaf herself. Supported by Skipper, her hearing dog, and concentrating totally, Kerena produced notes that were every bit as full as those completed by hearing people. But it took its toll. By the end of the day, Kerena was exhausted, although Skipper was still full of bounce and vitality.

Deaf people never receive the support they deserve. They're often treated as daft or, at the very least, as an irritation.

Yet many of us who are physically hearing can be spiritually and emotionally deaf. We shut our ears to the cries of those people we don't want to hear. We block out sounds that we find discordant. We turn a deaf ear to situations that might disturb us. We judge a situation from our perspective but are not prepared to listen in order to appreciate the other person's.

Nor are we just deaf to the needs of others. We're often deaf to the word and the will of God. It takes too much effort. It demands too much concentration. And so, rather than set aside the necessary time, we pretend lines to God are engaged and we're not prepared to hang on.

Listening to God isn't easy. We may not always like what we hear, but unless we're prepared to listen, we'll wander through life cut off from all things spiritual. Spiritual deafness is as great a disability as physical deafness.

All or nothing

Apparently the way to deal with modern living is to put everything into different compartments. Home life in one, work in another. Hobbies should be kept separate from duties. Holiday finances need to be in a different pocket from household running costs. Personal friends and work colleagues should be kept well apart. And it follows that weekly worship should be divorced from everyday life. If you follow this advice, some people believe that not only will your life be happy and contented, it will also be successful.

I'm not so sure. I firmly believe that one part of your life influences another. And that's how it should be. Life is so much easier if some of our workmates can also be friends, and it makes sense if our hobbies help us relax and give us strength to do our daily work. If we're unhappy at home, it's bound to affect the way we work. When a child is being bullied at school, it always has a knock-on effect at home. We can't live our lives in separate compartments. We're not made like that. It's not natural.

Of course, people who separate their religious beliefs from the way they actually behave are open to accusations of hypocrisy. A faith that is a Sunday-only sensation is worthless. After all, people expect you to put your money where your mouth is. There's little point in singing hymns about love if your heart is full of hate.

God commanded us that we should love him with all our heart, with all our soul, with all our mind and with all our strength. A belief that is purely intellectual or solely emotional is incomplete. It really should be a matter of all or nothing.

Just as that's true about belief, so it must be true about life as a whole. Putting parts of your life into different, separate compartments fragments it and, in the end, makes it very difficult. And it certainly doesn't help in our relationships with other people. What they want is all of you – and that's exactly what God wants as well.

The silent killer

To be honest, I have very little time for surveys. I find some of them fascinating, but I really do question their value. Has your opinion ever been sought? Mine certainly hasn't. But statistics are rather different. I know you can make statistics mean whatever you want them to mean, but these particular statistics really did strike a chord with me. In Britain today, 4.8 million women and 3.3 million men are living alone. So it's no wonder that loneliness is an ever-growing problem.

Obviously, not everyone who lives alone is lonely. In fact, loneliness is as different from solitude as starving is from fasting. One kills, the other revives. Loneliness and solitude are two totally different experiences. One is harmful, the other can be fulfilling.

We all need to be able to live with solitude. It's the mark that we're at peace with ourselves and are able to live with ourselves. Nothing could be more strengthening.

Jesus got great comfort from being alone. From that solitude came the strength to cope with the rest of his very demanding life. Only twice during his life do we get even the slightest glimpse of any possible loneliness, and that loneliness is soon overcome by the firm knowledge of the presence of God.

Loneliness is a killer. I believe it's far more destructive than cancer, and it's more prevalent. It may not kill the body but it certainly can kill the mind and the soul. And it can only be cured when it's faced up to.

It's no good pretending that you're not lonely if all you have is an aching heart. Your readiness to face your own loneliness can be the first step on the road to recovery. From then on, it's a matter of determination. Make yourself meet people. Make yourself take an interest in other people. Make yourself become a more interesting person. Don't be judgmental of others. In fact, don't even be judgmental of yourself – and who knows, your loneliness could well become solitude. Your weakness could become your strength.

Keeping in touch

At one time when I arrived home, having been away for a couple of days, there was just the post to pick up from the mat. These days, not only is there the post to attend to but also the messages on the telephone answering machine, faxes and e-mail correspondence.

I mustn't complain. There are some people who long for the postman to call, even if it's only with junk mail.

There's no excuse for not finding the time to keep in touch. A quick phone call at the right time can be very cheap. One or two lines scribbled on a notelet takes only a few minutes. And yet, apart from Christmas time, most of us fail miserably.

When I was a boy away at school I received a letter from my mother every Monday afternoon, and she expected me to reply. If I didn't, she wanted to know why. That discipline has stood me in good stead ever since. My letters meant a lot to my mother and so did her letters to me.

It isn't just the pace of life today that stops us from keeping in touch, it's often a case of sheer thoughtlessness. Because our lives are busy and interesting, we forget about those people who are shut in, unable to get out, or just lonely. A letter through the door would make all the difference. It's even better than a phone call. A letter you can read and reread. A phone call is with you one minute and gone the next. Phone calls can also be frustrating. No sooner have you put the receiver down than you remember a hundred and one things you meant to say.

It's not just other people whom we need to maintain contact with. We also need to keep in touch with God. Again, we can make the time. Our regular prayers and Bible reading take us out of ourselves and make us realize our dependence on God. But cut off communication with him and you're truly living in a world of your own.

Bringing much comfort

It's an awkwardness we've all faced. How should you respond when someone has been bereaved? Do you send a card, write a letter or pick up the telephone? The reaction of most people is to panic. Frightened they may say the wrong thing, they say nothing at all. Even those who decide to write are often left wondering what exactly to say and when to say it.

During my time as a priest I've tried to comfort many people who've been bereaved, and the one thing I've noticed is that every single person is different. While one wants to talk a lot, another wants silence. While one fills every minute with activity, another just can't get started on anything. So at an early age, I learnt there were no hard and fast rules about how to care for those who are bereaved. After all, the death of a 93-year-old who has led a full and purposeful life generates a different reaction from that of a father leaving a young widow with young children.

Nor would you say the same thing to someone whose child has died as you would to someone who has lost a wife after a long illness. One death is cruelly out of time whereas the other may be a merciful relief.

Recently I was reading a book written by a father about the death of his son. When it came to the question of how to comfort the bereaved, he had some very good advice. He wrote simply, 'Be honest, be brief, be there.'

Honesty is vital if you're going to offer worthwhile comfort. Say what you really believe, not what you think you ought to say. If you're angry, say so.

But don't write pages and pages in a letter or stay for hours when you visit. Several short visits are of much greater help and support. And finally, just be available whenever you're needed. Someone who can always be relied on is worth their weight in gold.

Where we belong

Have you ever wondered where you came from and to whom you belong? Well, wonder no longer. Help is at hand. The Church of the Latter Day Saints, more commonly known as the Mormons, has come to the rescue, posting a database on the Internet providing details of 400 million people going back to the mid-15th century. But don't worry if you can't find your family. A further 200 million names will soon be added.

The thinking behind this for the Mormons is that unbaptized ancestors can be brought into their fold. However, for most people it will be a way of checking on the branches – or roots – of their family tree. The world of genealogical research has become a fast-growing hobby. Over an eight-week test period of the database, 200 million people accessed it. But then I shouldn't be surprised, as tracing family history has become one of the most popular uses of the Internet.

Tracing your family is, of course, nothing new. You only have to look at the first chapter of St Matthew's Gospel to find yourself in a forest of 'begats'. 'Abraham begat Isaac, Isaac begat Jacob' and so on, until you eventually get to: 'Jacob begat Joseph, the husband of Mary, who gave birth to Jesus the Messiah.' It was vital for any first-century Jew to be able to trace Jesus' lineage back to both David and Abraham if they were to accept him as the Messiah.

This sense of belonging has always been a basic need of the human race. We want to know that we're part of a family, that we have roots – because it's in times of difficulty that we return to those roots.

As children of God, we also belong to his family. It is to God that we ultimately belong. So the next time you think, 'I don't seem to belong to anyone', think again. And don't be worried if you're not into the Internet. A prayer will do.

Put on a pedestal

Just behind London's busy Oxford Street lies Cavendish Square. It's a lovely green oasis in the heart of the West End. In the middle of the garden square there's a pedestal on which there's no statue. I've often wondered who I might like to put on it. Should it be a member of the great and the good? Or should it be one of the hundreds of people I know who may not be regarded as great but who, in my eyes, are certainly very good indeed?

Then I have second thoughts. It's far better for the pedestal to remain empty. Because the moment you put someone on a pedestal, you run into difficulties.

This was exactly what Judas did to Jesus. Judas had fixed ideas of exactly what the Messiah would be like. For one thing, he would rid Israel of the Roman army of occupation. But when he discovered that Jesus wasn't that sort of Messiah, his whole world fell apart.

This happens time and time again when we put people on pedestals. No sooner are they lifted up than someone tries to drag them down. It's a mistake to put any human being in such a position. We all have weaknesses. We all have feet of clay. And sooner or later, even the most marvellous human beings are seen to have chinks in their armour.

I'm sure that the people who are put on pedestals themselves would be the first ones to acknowledge that they're not perfect. The late Diana, Princess of Wales, was put on a pedestal, a position she found both frightening and lonely. That's because pedestals are lonely, frightening places. So she made sure she came off hers as frequently as possible. She came to the level of everyone she met and yet there were still people determined to push her back where they, mistakenly, thought she belonged – on a pedestal.

Putting parents or partners on pedestals is never wise. They, too, are only human and in time they will feel the pressure or they will be thought to have let you down. There's only one person for whom a pedestal is appropriate and that is God. Perfection can't be pulled off a pedestal, however hard we try.

Food for thought

Before you say anything, I'll come clean. Yes, I'm back on my old hobby-horse, the family meal. But it's not my fault. I blame Oxo. Recently they decided that the time had come for 'the last supper'. The casserole dishes were packed away, the kitchen was emptied and, with the words, 'time to go', the award-winning Oxo television adverts came to an end.

For 21 years there's been an Oxo family enjoying a meal together on our television screens, but the family meal has lost out to the pre-cooked meal. With the rise in the number of women with jobs outside the home, fewer parents and children sit down together to eat. It won't be that long before dining tables are declared obsolete and children will wander around museums asking what those funny hunks of wood on legs were for.

Our lifestyles have changed. The demands on our time are greater for us all. But I still don't think that it's beyond the capability of any family to eat together at least once a week. The meal table is such a crucial meeting place. The views of the different generations can be heard. Children keep in touch with their parents and parents hear in a relaxed way about the interests, achievements and disappointments of their children. The end of the family meal has done more damage to family life than anything else.

Meals aren't just for our physical needs; they sustain us spiritually and emotionally as well, bringing people together. That's why meals figure so prominently in religions.

The key meal for Jews is the Passover Meal. The central meal for Christians is the Last Supper. Both these meals brought together, and continue to bring together, families and friends, and both are far more than food and drink. They are deeply spiritual experiences, when people look back at times past with thanksgiving and forward to the future with hope.

Pre-cooked meals will feed us physically, but emotionally and spiritually we shall be left to starve.

10

Love and Acceptance

It worries some people, annoys others and reassures the rest. I have chosen one of the hymns for my funeral. It is Charlotte Elliott's *Just as I am, without one plea* – and I want it sung to the tune of 'Saffron Walden'. It is not only the listeners to Radio 2's *Sunday Half Hour* who have favourites. The presenter has as well!

'Just as I am', based on Psalm 139, is for me the most wonderful expression of the Christian faith. It is about love and it is about acceptance. You can take any verse, but let's just take verse 4:

Just as I am, thou wilt receive,
Wilt welcome, pardon, cleanse, relieve:
Because thy promise I believe,
O Lamb of God I come.

So much of the love that people experience is earned love. They have done everything in their power to make themselves loveable. Either they have been always willing to do things or they have made themselves a joy to be with or they have even gone to the gym and bought designer clothes. All in an attempt to make themselves accepted. Sadly, in the long term it rarely works.

The people who receive unearned love from the moment they are born have been given the greatest of all possible gifts. That gift mirrors the love that God has for us. His love is free, unearned and sustained, something that those people who haven't experienced such unconditional love in their personal lives find hard to accept. But accept it we must if we are to survive.

There were times when Jesus showed that there was a disciplined side to love. It wasn't always a matter of 'there, there'. It was sometimes 'Stop that'. But nevertheless there was an underpinning acceptance that meant that you were not rejected because you had done something wrong. Like the prodigal son, you could turn again and live. Love is our life-blood. Without it we are lost. With it we have the strength to live life to the full and, what is more, bring wholeness into the lives of others.

We all need hugs

Far be it from me to criticize modern medicine, but at times it does have rather uncomfortable side-effects. My friend Juliet has been having a grim time lately. No one's entirely sure what's wrong with her, despite the enquiring minds of many doctors in several hospitals.

Recently she was admitted for further tests. Sadly, because of the distance and my work schedule, I wasn't able to visit her. So I phoned. 'How are you?' I asked. 'Fine,' she replied bravely, 'except that at the moment I'm radioactive, so the order of the day is No Hugs.'

I could think of nothing crueller. Juliet is an outgoing, friendly person and heavily into hugs. 'No hugs' was, for her, more a torture than a cure.

There's something very special about a hug. It's a way of loving someone and protecting them at the same time. The child who grows up without being hugged is heading for unhappiness. Hugging isn't sexual, or it needn't be. It's a way of saying, 'I love you, I want to be with you and I want to protect you.'

A hug says more than a thousand words, especially at times of great crisis and distress. So to be denied that source of comfort and strength when sick and uncertain is terribly harsh.

When Jesus wanted to show his care and concern for children, he 'took them into his arms and blessed them'. He hugged them. Sadly, because of the current climate, you have to be so careful about children. Your own children, grandchildren and Godchildren certainly deserve a hug and it's wonderful when they hug you as well.

Mary Magdalene suffered the sharp pain of rejection when she was told by Jesus that first Easter, 'Do not touch me.' She too was a hugging person and the sight of her risen Lord must have made her want to reach out in love and joy. But at that time it was a case of 'no hugs'. Whatever you do, hang on to hugs and don't deny them to the people you love or those you want to protect.

Depend on me

'Goodness only knows how you'd manage without me.' If I had a pound for every time I've heard that, I'd be a very rich man indeed.

People who've sewn on buttons for me, people who've organized Sunday School outings for me, people who've come to my rescue when I haven't had time to do the shopping, have all uttered those very words. On one occasion I even forgot I'd invited people for dinner. A friend set to work at the last minute and supplied the whole meal!

Clearly I couldn't manage without others, although I realized a long time ago that people could get on quite well without me. However, this knowledge hasn't stopped me, at times, wanting to make myself indispensable. I've tried to make people so dependent on me that, without my help or advice, they'd find life difficult. But in the end I've realized that it's not good for them and it's not good for me either.

Making myself indispensable is a way of meeting *my* needs rather than those of the person I'm supposed to be helping. It may appear to work in the short term but it certainly won't over a long period of time.

This was the painful lesson that even Moses had to learn. Leading the Children of Israel out of Egypt hadn't been easy. He'd sorted out the minor inconvenience of the Red Sea but still he was beset by the disagreements and disputes of his people. Hour after hour he listened to them, trying to solve their troubles, until his father-in-law pointed out that if he continued in that way he'd wear himself out and be absolutely no use to anybody.

He needed to delegate, to appoint others to take on some of the burden, those who were equally skilled at resolving quarrels. Moses could then concentrate on the various tasks he had to complete, and at the same time allow others to blossom into responsibility.

We all need to be needed, but we should never forget that allowing others to be independent is far more important than making ourselves indispensable.

That's the way I am

Imagine the scene. A mother and her young teenage son were shopping and the trolley was piled high, along with extra carrier bags. At least there were two pairs of hands to tackle the problem; the only trouble was that the son wanted to keep hold of the lolly he was sucking. Every so often he'd thrust his lolly at his mum for her to have a lick. But she didn't want to and soon her son's behaviour began to annoy her. Finally, in sheer exasperation, I heard her say, 'For goodness' sake, can't you behave!' To which he replied, 'No, Mum. That's the way I am.'

What a cop-out. This boy wasn't totally irresponsible or he wouldn't have been lending his mother a hand with the shopping, but he'd learnt at an early age to opt out of all responsibility for his actions. However, it won't work.

Unless there's a genuine medical reason for unreasonable behaviour, we have to take responsibility for the way we are. Life is harder for some than others, but that doesn't give anyone the right to act in any way they want.

I always think it's insulting to people who are unemployed to suggest unemployment is a cause of social unrest. The majority of unemployed people wouldn't dream of stealing or mugging: all they want is a job and to regain their self-respect. However, a minority do use unemployment as an excuse for irresponsible behaviour and, once again, it won't wash.

Although we're made in the image of God, we know we've fallen from grace. More often than not our actions are led by our own selfishness. We have a responsibility to run our lives so we become more like him, and we'll never do that if we're unwilling to take responsibility for who we are or what we do. So the next time you are taken to task for your behaviour, please don't say, 'Sorry, but that's the way I am.'

Sweet charity

Where does charity really begin? I have to admit that if it hadn't been for a charity my early years would have been even more difficult. And not just for me, for my widowed mother as well. My father was a clergyman who died when I was one. Within three months of his death we had to be out of the vicarage, find a new home and re-establish ourselves. There was no social security to cushion the blow and there was no pension to sustain the future. If we were to survive my mother had to get a job.

She became a teacher – which in those days was a low-paid job. Running a home and bringing up two young boys took every penny she earned. To the rescue came a charity with the rather forbidding name, 'The Clergy Orphan Corporation'. They paid for my brother and me to go to a school where not only were we educated but fed and, to a certain extent, clothed as well.

Not everyone would agree with sending their children away to school, but for my mother it was a terrific help. It meant that for eight months of the year not only were we fed and watered, but we had a male influence in our lives too – something that would have been missing if we'd stayed at home. At school we were called 'Foundationers' and we were proud of it. It even meant that we got a little extra pocket money on special occasions. Certainly there was nothing to be ashamed of. If anything, we were proud that a charity had come to our rescue. But I have to admit that charities and those who receive charity hand-outs do not always get such a good name.

'As cold as charity' and 'Charity begins at home' are two phrases that come quickly to many people's minds, even at harvest time when, rather like Christmas, they are often feeling a bit more generous. And yet a charitable attitude and charitable giving are at the heart of all faiths, not only the Christian one, although Jesus, by his life, put a lot of emphasis on it. 'There are three things that last for ever: faith, hope and charity; but the greatest of these is charity,' writes St Paul.

I know that modern translations use the word 'love' rather than 'charity', but the two words are interchangeable. Certainly charity without love is very cold indeed. When people adopt the attitude that 'charity begins at home', it generally means that it stays at home. They are not prepared to look further than their immediate needs and the needs of those close to them. But when people give or receive charity with a generous or grateful heart, it becomes very sweet indeed.

Broken vows

What's happening to married Britain? With almost 40 per cent of marriages ending in divorce, Britain has the highest divorce rate in Europe. What's more, as things stand at the moment it can only get worse. Which means there will be even more casualties.

It's very hard to survive a divorce completely unscathed. Husband and wife suffer a sense of failure and guilt. In-laws and friends are forced into taking sides, and children are left wondering who they can really trust.

Some people believe that making divorce less agonizing is the only hope. I don't. Nor do I think that pre-marital contracts would help. They certainly couldn't minimize the pain for the children.

Of course, I wouldn't wish even more anguish on anyone going through divorce. But if only they'd been given a little more help before they married, they might have been better prepared for the stresses and strains that came later.

Getting people to think seriously about what they're committing themselves to before they marry isn't easy. They're so euphoric. They're in love and all they want to think about is the dress, the reception and the honeymoon. But somehow a sense of reality must be brought into this make-believe world. I don't want to be the wicked witch but I feel it's vital to point out the pitfalls as well as the pleasures.

What's needed is a change in attitude from society as a whole. We've lost our sense of commitment. Everything and everybody has become disposable. Loyalty is a thing of the past. Why should people about to get married be any different from the rest of society? If we don't have or support those values why should we expect them of others?

This is nothing new. Moses faced problems of commitment with the Children of Israel; Jesus did with his disciples. It will only be when everyone has a greater understanding of commitment that they will be able to overcome and live through some of the difficulties that, these days, lead all too quickly to divorce.

Facing the facts

The only thing that marred the start of my summer holidays from boarding school was the dreaded end-of-year report. It usually arrived through the letterbox two days after I'd come home. One particular year it was even more threatening. Along with the report was a letter from my headmaster. I feared the worst.

I stood nervously by my mother's side as she read it out. The first paragraph was encouraging: Mr Cox loved my performance in the school play. Then my mother fell silent. Being the inquisitive lad I was, I looked over her shoulder and tried to read the letter for myself.

I soon saw the reason for her silence. I was not about to be expelled. It was simply that Mr Cox wanted to inform my mother that he had given me a talk on the facts of life.

Being a widow, I think my mother breathed a sigh of relief. Her responsibilities had been taken care of and there was now no need for sex ever to be mentioned again in our house.

As I recall, Mr Cox's talks were sensible and informative – although, like other boys, I'd heard most of it before from my mates in the playground. However, I appreciated being told in an easy-to-understand manner by someone I really respected.

So I was surprised to hear the recent suggestion that teen publications should do this sensitive job. I expect there are many teenagers who would prefer to learn about sex from magazines rather than from their parents or teachers. But since in the past some of these magazines have been criticized for 'squalid titillation, salaciousness and smut', are we sure they're the best guides for our young people?

We're told that our bodies are 'the temple of the Holy Spirit', and I believe it's far better for children to find out about sexual matters from someone they respect and can question openly and honestly. And it should be made clear that sex isn't just a collection of physical functions; the necessary information needs to be conveyed within the context of human relationships at their deepest level.

Sharing the load

Hidden disabilities can often be harder to bear than obvious ones. If you see someone carrying a white stick you know they're blind. Someone who's in a wheelchair is clearly unable to walk. But unless a person is wearing a visible hearing aid, there is no immediate way of knowing whether he or she is deaf.

Another hidden disability is epilepsy. My nephew Stephen had it. Although it frustrated him, he never let it dominate his life. However, epilepsy is a very cruel condition. You never know when it will strike, and if other people know that you have it, they're often nervous of being in your company.

Drugs have enabled many epileptics to lead full lives, but still a shadow hangs over them. And that shadow will only be removed when those of us who don't suffer from epilepsy show more understanding towards those who do.

Sadly, Stephen died suddenly and tragically only a short while ago. He was a mature student at Oxford and, having just suffered the ordeal of taking his final exams, he and a friend went for a gentle punt on the river Cherwell. As he took over the punting pole, he had a fit, fell into the river and drowned.

On the morning of his funeral I was doing *Pause for Thought* on Radio 2. I talked about Stephen, his life, his faith and his epilepsy. Very kindly, a lot of listeners, many of whom were *Woman's Weekly* readers, wrote to me. I shall always treasure those letters, especially the ones that came from fellow epilepsy sufferers. It took courage for them to write, but they reveal a sensitivity only they could show.

They were doing precisely what St Paul had instructed the Galatians to do: 'Carry one another's burdens.' Having listened to me, they realized I was feeling sad and in need of support. By writing a letter, sending a card, making a phone call, they were reaching out a helping hand and a listening ear.

We all need support and encouragement, and it's our duty to offer these to others when we can. No one should have to bear a burden alone.

Reclaiming our morals

The fact that the United Kingdom has the highest rate of teenage pregnancies in Europe amazed me. But I wasn't surprised that with news of the latest 12-year-old mother, came cries of horror and a call for a moral crusade. More responsible parents and better sex education in schools are seen as the key to getting Britain back on the moral track. They will help, but it'll take much more than that.

If we are to create a new sense of morality, then we must realize that morals mean more than sex. Immorality hasn't always meant sexual immorality. If you read the New Testament gospels, you'll read a great deal about morals but very little about sex. Jesus has more to say about how we treat the poor, how we use our money and how we criticize others than he does about our sex lives. So we should realize that sex is only part of the moral problem.

Morality is about the way in which we treat each other, and it all stems from the way in which we treat ourselves.

If you haven't a proper respect for yourself, there's little chance you'll respect others. A 12-year-old who gets pregnant and a 14-year-old who gets her pregnant can have little respect for themselves, let alone each other. But they certainly won't be helped to get a greater sense of morality by a society that's dominated by greed, gain and constant gratification; a society that's put respect on the back burner.

Of course, respect must be part of sex, but so must it be part of our financial dealings, our sense of commitment to those we love and our sense of responsibility to those less fortunate than ourselves. We're just as immoral when we let someone down emotionally as we are when we use someone sexually.

Let's help people to respect themselves, then they will automatically respect others and the moral high ground will have been reclaimed.

In on the act

For years, I thought that I was the only member of the family to hit the headlines, be on the box and ride the airwaves – until I discovered that my 89-year-old Auntie Do was at it as well. The local freebie newspaper had managed to get an exclusive. Posing with a glass in her hand, Auntie Do was ready to tell the world that her hip replacement was 30 years old. There are some older hip replacements, but very few.

Given the opportunity to tell the world – well, the Prestwich area of Manchester – my aunt wanted to thank the surgeon who had pioneered the operation, the hospital that had done a wonderful job and the NHS for making such a life-transforming operation available even to those without pots of money. And not one to waste an opportunity, she also wanted to encourage those people who were in need of the operation to 'go for it'.

This, to me, was a very refreshing story. Today we're more likely to sue our doctors than thank them. Or at best we take them for granted unaware of the demands and pressures put upon them.

It seems as if nothing has changed since Jesus healed the ten lepers. These outcasts of society were met by Jesus. Standing at a distance, afraid to come near, they begged for pity. Jesus advised them to go and show themselves to the priests. As they were going, they were healed. Nine continued on their journey. Only one, a foreigner, took the trouble to turn back to Jesus and thank him.

Thanks often comes from the least expected quarters. Often the person who has much expects more. The dissatisfied person tends to be disgruntled whatever you give them. It's only the person who expects little who is genuinely grateful for all they receive, be it big or small. And what's more, they're prepared to share their gratitude with others. I hope you come under that category.

Which way?

The lady in the newspaper kiosk outside the Lambeth North London Undergound station is obviously fed up with directing people to the Imperial War Museum. Above her kiosk is a hand-written sign: 'No directional advice given here.' I don't blame her. And yet it must be very frustrating for visitors desperate to find one of London's most interesting museums, for when you step out of the Underground station it's far from clear which way to turn.

'Directional advice' is something I'm constantly in need of – and never more so than at the start of a new year. One of the titles Jesus gave himself was 'I am the Way', so it seems he was only too willing to give directional advice.

To the woman caught in the act of adultery he said, 'Go and sin no more.' When the rich young man wanted to know how he could get eternal life, Jesus told him to go and sell all he had and follow him. To the lawyer who wanted to know who was his neighbour, he told the parable of the Good Samaritan.

These were clear directions given in answer to direct questions, but the most direct question of all that Jesus answered was, 'Which is the first commandment of all?' This came from a scribe, who would have known his Jewish Scriptures well. And the advice given was, 'The first is, "You shall love the Lord your God with all your heart and with all your soul and with all your mind and with all your strength." And the second is, "You shall love your neighbour as yourself." There is no other commandment greater than these.'

So if you're looking for directional advice you couldn't do better than accept the directions given by Jesus. Look at the way in which you show your love to God. Are you grateful for the many blessings he has given you or do you just turn to him in times of need? How well are you getting on with your family and neighbours? Should you show them more love? And what about yourself: are you giving yourself the love you need? These are the questions you need to ask yourself if you want to face in the right direction.

It goes without saying

Although actions may speak louder than words, there are times when words are still very important. The look in the eyes, the clasp of the hands, the fondness of an embrace may well show that two people are very much in love, but these actions must be supported by words. It isn't a matter of 'either, or'. It's a case of both.

Words without actions can be hollow, but however much we show our love and affection, we need to tell people how much they mean to us. It's no good thinking, 'It goes without saying.' It doesn't. It needs to be said.

Recently the father of a friend of mine died. For days his wife was distraught and kept asking, 'Do you think he knew that I loved him? Did he really know?' All because she hadn't actually told him. He did know, of course, but how sad that she should have been left with anguish and doubt.

What's true in marriage is also true in friendship. We need to be told that we're loved. We need to tell others that we love them. Throughout my life I've had friendships that have meant a tremendous amount to me. People who have seen me through difficult times. People with whom I've shared success. It's only by telling friends how much their honesty, faithfulness and trust mean to you that you can be sure they know you love them.

At the end of St John's account of the gospel story, he records a very tender if somewhat difficult meeting between Peter and Jesus. Yes, Peter had denied Jesus during his trials but now, once again, Peter was accepted. He was one of the first at the empty tomb. He was there on the first Easter night when Jesus appeared to the disciples. He even shared breakfast with Jesus by the Sea of Galilee. But for Jesus there was still something missing. He needed Simon Peter to declare his love. Three times Jesus asked, 'Simon, son of John, do you love me more than all else?' It can't have been easy for Peter. In fact, he felt hurt. But if Peter was to carry out the work that Jesus had in mind for him, it needed to be said. He had to say that he loved Jesus as well as show it.

Putting feelings into words isn't easy. For some it's very embarrassing, but unless you do it, you're missing out on a vital part of friendship and you could be storing up regrets for the future. Go on, say it: 'I love you.'

'I don't believe it!'

I'm becoming more like Victor Meldrew every day – grumpy, cantankerous and caustic. I'm also finding some things very difficult to believe. No, don't worry, I'm not having difficulties with my faith in God. But I am having very real difficulties with my faith in my fellow human beings.

In the street where I live we're quite neighbourly, so I wasn't surprised when a note from the man at number 12 came through the door. The York-stone paving slabs outside his house had disappeared and he thought we ought to know why. They hadn't been removed by workers from Water, Gas, Phone or Cable as we all assumed. They'd been stolen. And in broad daylight. How it was done, goodness only knows. These stones aren't light. You would have thought that someone would have seen them being removed. But no one had.

The local council expressed little surprise. Apparently it had happened before. We were just warned to be on the look-out so that the thieves didn't come back for more paving slabs.

Fortunately, the council had a few spare stones so the pavement was returned to its former glory. But it's the sheer cheek that gets me.

I was staggered when a teenager walking along in front of me suddenly decided that she no longer wanted the large plastic milk container that she was carrying. So, in front of her mother, she just threw it on the ground. After I commented, she did have the grace to pick it up. But why didn't her mother say something? People these days do what they want, when they want and heaven help anyone who ever tries to correct them. I don't believe it!

Yet if we are going to survive, we have to believe in people. We have to trust one another. I know that Jesus tried it with his disciples and failed with some of them. However, he never stopped trusting. His faith in human nature never wavered. He was even prepared to take risks with people, such as Peter, who'd already let him down, and Paul, who'd taken great delight in persecuting the early Christians. They were given another chance to show they could be trusted.

In the same way as the father welcomed back the prodigal son, so God welcomes us back. He never loses faith in us. So we should do our best never to lose faith in other people, although, at certain times, it will be very hard.

Mutton dressed as lamb

I can't say I'm ever surprised by reports that find that creams designed to remove the signs of ageing are not all they're cracked up to be. But some people will never give up. They're prepared to have their faces doused with chemicals and swathed in bandages so that, at the final unveiling, they can appear younger than their birth certificate tells them they are. Why they don't just alter the birth certificate and take the pretence even further, I'll never know. It would certainly be cheaper, and far less painful on the skin and the pocket.

Growing old can be upsetting. Eyes and ears don't work so well. Hips and knees seem to creak more. Everything takes that bit longer to do. But there are plusses. You're not in such a rush. More of your time is your own. And you have all that experience of life behind you. That's got to be good.

The Bible didn't always get ages right by our way of calculating – in those days, people tended to add years rather than subtract them. To them, old age was a privilege, not a distinct disadvantage. The older members of the tribe or the family were held in great respect, awe and affection. They certainly weren't seen as a burden or a nuisance.

It was to the elderly that Jesus was first revealed as Christ. There was nothing glamorous about Simeon or Anna as they waited day after day in the Temple. They weren't mutton dressed as lamb. I would imagine that their skin looked like dried up parchment. But behind that skin were hearts and spiritual insights that were as fresh as ever.

The sooner we get back respect for the elderly, the better. And as you grow old, don't worry about the anti-ageing creams or the facelifts. Keep the heart and the mind young. That, in the end, is what will show.

Judged by computer

This summer I spent a couple of days in Northumbria. The weather was glorious and the scenery magnificent. I was staying with Rachel, my eldest Goddaughter, and her family. Husband Mike had left for work and Rachel had taken their son, Sam, to Newcastle for a much-needed haircut. Daughter Jessica and I were left to look after the home. I needed to do some writing and Jessica decided to play games on her computer. Every so often I heard a strange noise from the computer.

'What's that?' I asked.

'Oh, it's just the computer telling me I've scored a point,' Jessica replied.

Soon the computer gave a sound like a deep sigh.

'What's up now?'

'The computer doesn't think I'm doing terribly well,' she said.

Judgement by computer, I thought. That's all you need!

Being judged by fellow human beings is bad enough, but when machines start doing it you stand very little chance indeed. Pleading your case in front of other people you can at the very least claim mitigating circumstances, or ask for matters to be taken into consideration before judgement is passed. With machines you are either guilty or not guilty.

Some people, however, pass judgement without knowing all the facts, and that can be equally terrifying and totally unjust. One reason why I think there is no need to fear the judgement of God is because his judgement is both fair and honest. The fact that God 'knows the very secrets of our hearts' and yet still loves us should make us feel secure. The only time to be frightened is when we know we're deliberately going against God's will; when for us, there are no extenuating circumstances and we are hell-bent on wickedness.

Free will is the greatest gift we have from God. As each of us is unique, different factors affect the way in which we exercise that free will.

Someone who has pots of money experiences different pressures from a person who is poor. The strong man's (or woman's) concerns are different from those of someone who is weak.

All this is taken into account by God before passing judgement. Machines cannot do this and other human beings don't bother.

But we must remember that gifts never come without responsibilities. And it's our responsibility to use the gift of free will to the best of our ability and circumstances. God doesn't, and won't, expect more from us.